A Greenpatch Book

Dirty, Rotten, Dead?

Written by Jerry Emory
Illustrated by T. Taylor Bruce

Who Is a Greenpatch Kid?

Anyone. Maybe you. All over the world, young people who care about the earth are doing things: helping to save habitats; protecting endangered animals; helping to clean up pollution. If *you* believe that humans need to take better care of the earth, and if you are ready to do your part, you may already be a Greenpatch Kid. For more information about the kids' environmental movement and how you can participate, see page 48.

A Gulliver Green Book
Harcourt Brace & Company
San Diego New York London

Library of Congress Cataloging-in-Publication Data is available on request. ISBN 0-15-200695-8

First edition A B C D E .

Gulliver Green® Books focus on various aspects of ecology and the environment, and a portion of the proceeds from the sale of these books will be donated to protect, preserve, and restore native forests. *A Greenpatch Book* is a registered trademark of Harcourt Brace & Company.

This book is dedicated to Greenpatch Kids everywhere.

Printed in Singapore

Some of the Things in This Book

P9-AGU-226

The Dead Parts of You

Your skin is amazing. Not only is it the most visible part of you, it is also your largest organ. Skin is packaging for your muscles and bones. It keeps your innards from spilling all over the floor. Skin breathes, perspires, and stretches. Your skin also helps you stay cool when it's hot, and warm when it's cold. And one last thing: *your skin is dead.*

That's right, the outermost layer of your skin, the *epidermis* (the stuff you touch and see), is made up of billions of dead skin cells that are constantly falling off, cell by cell. As your skin grows and falls off, it's replaced by new skin cells from below. Scabs, your skin's natural repair kits, are blood cells that die, then dry, over wounds. When the wounds heal, the scabs fall off.

your scalp

hair shaft

dead cells

2

dandruff and hair shafts

dead cells

epidermis

hair shaft

your skin

nerve

In fact, if you examine your body closely, you'll discover that many parts of you are dead and falling off. Take a hand lens and look at a dry patch of skin on your arm, a scab, or some hair. What you thought was simple is really quite complex. Does this fact make you scratch your head and wonder? If it does, what you are scratching *with* and what you are scratching *on* are also dead. Your fingernails (and your toenails) are very hard dead cells that are constantly being pushed out of your skin by the dead cells behind them. The dandruff that may have floated down to your shoulder is also dead. And the hairs on your head, and elsewhere on your body, are threadlike tubes of dead cells. Whether your hair is red, black, blond, or green, straight, short, curly, or spiked, it's all dead. And when you blow your nose, you will probably dislodge several chunks of dried (and dead) nose *mucus* that are packed with tiny particles of dust, dirt, and nose hairs.

The Dead Inside

But some dead parts of you are inside. Your urine is full of waste products from your blood system. Most of your urine is water your body couldn't use, but it also contains *urea* (a compound formed by the decomposition of protein) and a dash of salt. Your feces are packages of waste composed of dead *bacteria* (very important single-celled microorganisms), dead cells from your intestines, and tough fibers from meat and plants that you couldn't digest.

Discovering that parts of you are dead may be disturbing. (If it makes you anxiously gnash your teeth, then you're grinding enamel that is 98 percent dead!) You are very much alive and very much dead at the same time. In fact, if parts of you were not constantly dying, you would not grow. Death and life are *not* opposites. Dead and living things are dependent on each other. You can't have one without the other. That's what this book is all about.

So, wash your hands, comb your hair, clip your nails, brush your teeth, blow your nose, go to the bathroom, and shake off those dead cells. You have a lot of growing and living to do.

3

Follow the Bouncing Bolus

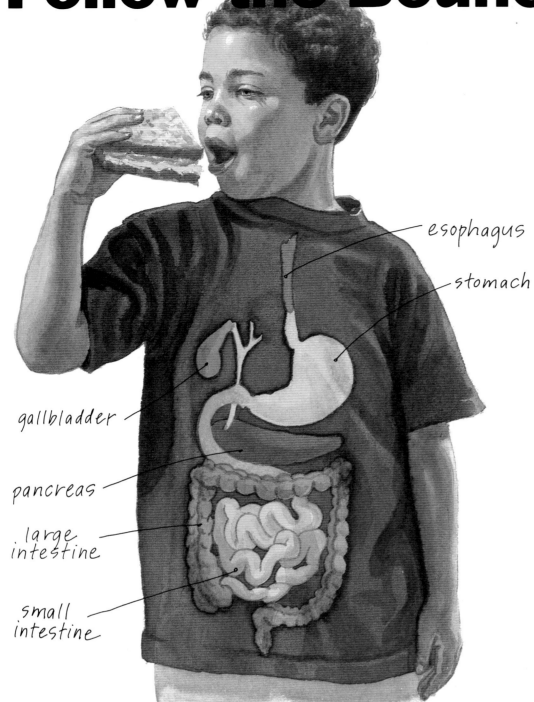

esophagus

stomach

gallbladder

pancreas

large intestine

small intestine

Esophagus

Once you swallow, the bolus enters your *esophagus*, the 10-inch tube that connects your mouth to your stomach. As the bolus enters your esophagus, your *glottis* (the opening to your lungs) closes so the bolus doesn't take a wrong turn and choke you. Your esophagus is wrapped in muscles that keep the tube closed unless a bolus or a swallow of liquid is on the way. When the esophagus detects a swallow, it opens and sends the bolus to the stomach with a series of small pushing waves called *peristaltic action*. It's not gravity that helps your food go down—it's your bolus surfing those esophageal waves. Without these waves, you wouldn't be able to eat or drink while lying down, or when you're hanging from your feet. (That's not a good idea, anyway.)

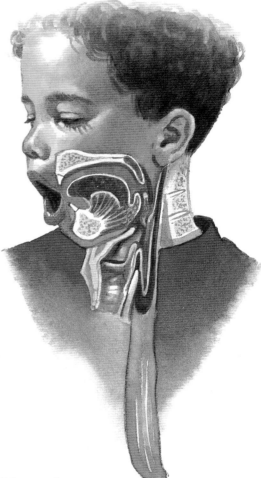

Stomach

When the bolus reaches your stomach, the real digestive work begins. Your stomach is a big hollow muscle that can hold about 3 pints of food (almost half a gallon). It contains hydrochloric acid and enzymes that help break down food. Your stomach is protected by a lining of mucus; otherwise it would digest itself! Your stomach contracts about every 20 seconds to turn and mix the *boli* (that's more than one bolus) with your digestive juices to produce a creamy food-fluid called *chyme*. Chyme is then squirted into the intestines at regular intervals. Sometimes when you are really hungry, or just when you see or smell food, your stomach "growls." That's your stomach producing digestive juices and beginning to contract and churn, just because you have been *thinking* about food.

Before they can produce waste (urine and feces), humans and other animals must eat food. Most animals have special diets. Wolves and lions are *carnivores* (meat eaters), while deer and horses are *herbivores* (plant eaters). Many birds, like flycatchers, are *insectivores* (insect eaters), while others, like finches, are *granivores* (seed and grain eaters). Flying foxes and toucans are *frugivores* (fruit eaters). You and some other animals—grizzly bears, for example—are *omnivores*. You can eat everything.

Your digestive system has adapted to what you get fed. Carnivores get protein and carbohydrates that have been eaten and digested by their prey. Every few days carnivores feast on huge amounts of meat that are easy for them to digest: they have big stomachs and short intestines. Herbivores convert energy stored in plant tissue to food their bodies can use. Herbivores must continuously eat small amounts of hard-to-digest plants: they have several small stomachs and very long intestines.

You are somewhere in the middle because you can eat a little of everything. Your digestive system is kind of between that of a lion and a horse. Here's how it works:

Mouth

Let's say you're eating a salami and lettuce sandwich on rye bread (meat, plant, and grain), a side dish of bananas (fruit), and chocolate-covered ants (insects). Take a small omnivorous bite and start chewing. All this food is smashed together, sliced by your teeth, and mixed with *saliva*. You call it spit, but saliva is really a weak acid full of *enzymes* (proteins that help break down food and begin the digestion inside your mouth).

As you chew, your mouth forms a *bolus* (a small lump of food). Now swallow and send the bolus on a journey that can take as long as a couple of days to complete while it moves some 30 feet through your digestive system!

Small Intestine

The small intestine is a food transfer station. It's here that nutrients are absorbed into your bloodstream and transported throughout your body. Your small intestine is coiled up inside your abdomen, but if you could stretch it out it would be about 20 feet long. It's called "small" because it's only about 1.5 inches in diameter.

Peeuuee-Pee

About 40 percent of people in the United States have a gene in their body that converts a sulfur compound in asparagus into a sulfurlike smell. (You know, the rotten egg smell.) Do you have this gene? Here's how to find out:

Cook some asparagus spears (boiled or steamed is nice, with a dollop of mayonnaise or creamy salad dressing). Eat them. Now, time how long it takes for the sulfur smell to come from your urine. This will tell you how fast your digestive system is. If you don't have this gene (then you are *lucky*), it's good to eat asparagus anyway, because it's packed with vitamins A, B_6, and C.

Eat a Beet and Turn Red

Beets get their beautiful purplish red color from a pigment called betanin. Some people's digestive systems can't process this pigment, so after eating beets their urine turns pink, and their feces look reddish! Check it out. Can you process betanin?

Cook some beets (boiled or steamed will do). Chow them down, you omnivore, you. Now, remember that food takes a while to move from your mouth to your rectum, so be patient. Check your urine first, and your feces later. Whether you see any red or not, beets are a great source of vitamin C (and, if you eat their green tops, you'll load up with beta-carotene, calcium, and iron).

The inside walls of your small intestine are packed with millions of *villi*, tiny fingerlike projections that absorb the nutrients inside your intestine and transfer them to your bloodstream. Each villus is covered with hundreds of microscopic hairlike microvilli that increase the absorption area of your small intestine to the size of a tennis court!

There are three parts to your small intestine: *duodenum*, *jejunum*, and *ileum*. The duodenum is the upper portion of this intestine. When food is present, it adds digestive enzymes that are produced from the liver, gallbladder, and pancreas. Beneficial bacteria living in your small and large intestines also help break down food. Food is then moved along by peristalsis to the jejunum (the middle section) for more refined digestion and absorption, and finally on to the ileum, where nutrients that escaped the duodenum and jejunum are absorbed.

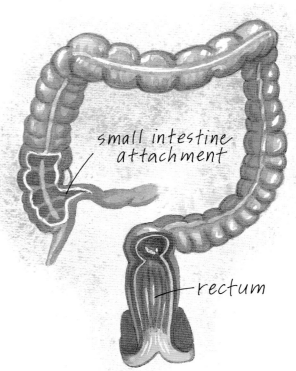

small intestine attachment

rectum

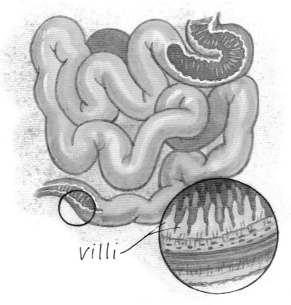

villi

Large Intestine

Your large intestine is only 5 feet long, but it's more than 2 inches in diameter (that's why it's called "large"). Food that isn't absorbed in your small intestine passes into the large intestine for more processing. Your large intestine has a smooth lining (instead of villi) that transfers nutrients and water into the bloodstream. Dead bacteria, dead cells from your intestines, and tough fibers from meat and plants are all packaged together here as feces. Feces are formed in the lower portions of your large intestine. They are then moved by peristalsis to your rectum and excreted.

layers of muscle

stomach lining

Down the Tubes

In order to live and grow, you must eat food and get rid of the dead parts of you. Two important ways that you remove these dead parts are by producing urine and feces. But what happens *after you* flush the toilet and your waste goes down the pipes? A hundred years ago North Americans didn't have to worry about flushing their toilets because their toilets didn't have handles. A hundred years ago a toilet was usually a seat positioned over a big hole in the ground. When the hole was full, the waste was covered with dirt, and the seat was moved to another hole! There are still plenty of toilets like these in the world.

Today, however, most toilets are connected to a system that collects human waste. The urine and feces you flush down the toilet combine with waste from sinks, showers, tubs, and washers from thousands of homes, apartments, and businesses. This combination of sewage and waste is called *wastewater*. Wastewater is processed at wastewater treatment plants. Most of these are designed to mimic how water is purified naturally in creeks, streams, and rivers. As water moves downstream, solid materials sink to the bottom, and the water is tossed about and mixed with oxygen. Aquatic plants and animals also help clean the water. Here is how a wastewater processing plant usually works:

Sewage Sleuth

Do you want to find out where your urine and feces end up? Ask for a tour of your local wastewater processing plant. How many gallons of wastewater does this plant process every day? How many stages does the wastewater go through before it is released? Where does the treated wastewater go? Does your local plant produce sludge, and if it does, who uses it?

6

Sun, Bacteria, and Algae

The remaining waste flows into more wastewater ponds, where it circulates with bacteria and *algae* (small aquatic plants). Working together, the bacteria and algae eat up any remaining organic matter in the wastewater. These ponds are open on top so the sunlight can help the algae stay alive and further clean the wastewater. Wastewater stays in these ponds for a month or more before going on to the next step.

From Your Intestines to a Stream

The next step in cleaning the wastewater mimics how streams and creeks clean water naturally. First, the algae and ammonia are removed, and the remaining wastewater is filtered by being passed over rocks or other structures in a tank, just as stream water passes over the rocks in a streambed. The wastewater is then mixed with the wastewater for about an hour to kill any remaining bacteria. However, before the wastewater is released into natural waterways (creeks, rivers, lakes, bays, oceans), sulfur dioxide is added to remove the chlorine, because chlorine is harmful to aquatic life. (Small amounts of sulfur dioxide don't hurt things living in the water.)

Out the End

Although it varies at each processing plant, most wastewater has had more than 95 percent of all pollutants removed by the time it leaves the plant. This final product is either discharged into nearby waterways or reused to irrigate grazing lands, golf courses, or the plants along highways.

Sludge and Scum

The wastewater continues its course into big containers called *settling tanks*. *Sludge* (organic solids) settles to the bottom, and a thin layer of *scum* (lighter waste, like grease and oil) floats to the top. The sludge is scraped off the bottom, mixed with the scum, and pumped to large *digester tanks* (these tanks are where the sludge and scum mixture, now just called sludge, is broken down). The remaining wastewater, almost free of solid stuff now, flows on to other wastewater ponds for further treatment.

Sludge Busters

There is no air inside the digester tanks, but there are plenty of bacteria, just like inside your intestines. Bacteria break down and consume most of the sludge. This bacteria feeding frenzy creates carbon dioxide and methane gas. The carbon dioxide is released into the atmosphere, but the methane gas is usually recycled to power the pumps and generators at the processing plant. The remaining sludge is either dried in large ovens heated by the methane gas or spread out on the ground and dried by the sun. Dried sludge is used as a soil fertilizer for landscape plants (not vegetables).

Troubled Waters

Wastewater treatment is far from perfect, and accidents and spills do occur. Some wastewater plants have a backup connection to the local storm drain system, and when there is a breakdown at the plant or there are heavy rains, raw sewage can flow into the nearest waterway. Treated and untreated wastewater can overload waterways with nutrients such as nitrogen and phosphorus. This supply of nutrients can result in an algae *bloom* (population explosion) that uses up the oxygen aquatic life needs to survive.

Septic Tanks

Some people who live in rural areas have a miniature wastewater treatment plant buried in their yard. It's called a septic tank. Septic tanks are made from wood, metal, plastic, or concrete. When wastewater enters the tank's first compartment, solids settle out and a scum layer forms on the top. Solids and scum are broken down by bacteria, just as they are in the digester tanks at wastewater plants. The wastewater then passes into a second compartment for more digestion before flowing through a series of underground drainpipes and into the ground.

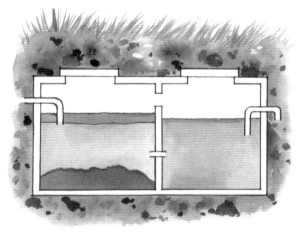

Compost Toilets

About 50 percent of your household water is used to flush toilets, unless you happen to have a compost toilet. Compost toilets look normal, but instead of flushing when you're done, you just close the lid. Your urine, feces, and toilet paper collect in a large insulated fiberglass tank, where they are digested by bacteria. A small fan brings oxygen to the bacteria while carrying away odors. Every six months, the bottom of the tank is opened, and the waste, now transformed into organic compost, is removed. It can be used as garden fertilizer, but it should not be put directly on vegetables.

natural cleansing

Storm Drain Pollution

Storm drain pollution is one of the primary sources of water pollution in the United States. It is pollution that *you* can help prevent.

During storms, rainwater moves over the surface of the ground and soaks into the soil. This natural filtering system cleans water *before* it reaches your local creek, river, or bay. But in most neighborhoods and cities, there are so many buildings, parking lots, and streets that rainwater can't soak into the ground. Instead, it flows downhill across pavement and concrete until it enters a storm drain and pours into your local waterway through an outfall pipe *without* being cleaned. Along the way, it may also pick up oil and pollutants from the streets. It carries waste that people dump into gutters and takes it all into the storm drains.

8

What's Going Where

It is impossible to figure out how your neighborhood storm drain system is laid out by just walking around on the streets. And don't even think about going into a storm drain—it's both *dangerous* and *illegal*. Instead, ask your city's public works department to help you study storm drains, their underground network of pipes, and find out where the outfall is located.

Any city or town that has a storm drain system will have someone at city hall with information about it. The public (that's you) is welcome to telephone the public works department, find out their business hours, then go look at their storm drain information.

The information you receive about storm drains can vary from city to city. Some public works departments have their system mapped out on computers, and they can print out the section you are interested in. Other departments will show you ancient maps with years of writing all over them. If this is the case, you may need to study the maps for a while and possibly ask a city engineer to help you understand them. It is also a good idea to see if you can photocopy them, or you can take notes and produce your own map when you get home.

storm drain run-off

no filtering of pollutants

Drain Brain

Adopt

After you've organized your group of drain brains and visited your city's public works department to ask for a copy of your local storm drain map, locate the storm drains around where you live, and mark them on your map. The number of drains you adopt will depend on the size of your group and how your storm drain system is built.

Stencil

Once you've identified several storm drains, start planning your stenciling program. Many cities around the U.S. already have storm drain stenciling programs. Your public works department should know. If they do, tell them you and your friends are interested in stenciling the storm drains in your neighborhood. They will help you get organized.

If your city doesn't have a stenciling program, here are some ideas you can take to your public works department for their consideration. Remember, you have to ask the city if it is OK to stencil storm drains.

Everything you need for stenciling can fit into a 5-gallon bucket. When stenciling, remember to wear clothes that can get dirty.

What you need:
your permit to stencil
your storm drain map
stencil (at right)
spray paint
wire brush and whisk broom
two trash bags
masking tape
paper towels or rags
disposable gloves for each member
traffic safety equipment: two orange-colored
  traffic cones and one orange vest for
  every member

How to Make a Stencil

What you need:
X-Acto knife with a sharp blade
two file folders or sheets of Mylar
ruler with a metal edge
grown-up assistant to help with cutting

1. Make as many photocopies of the design as you want stencils.

2. Tape the copy securely onto your file folder. Using your X-Acto knife and ruler (for the straight lines), cut out all the dark areas. Take your time and be careful. The small lines between the dark areas need to remain intact for the stencil to work properly.

3. Cut a rectangle out of the second file folder. Make it slightly larger than your message. This is your background shape.

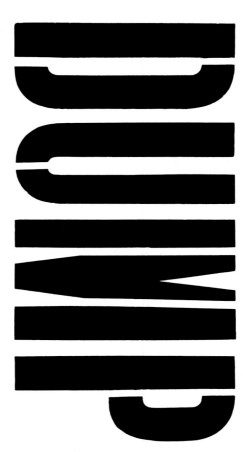

Paint Notes

Spray paint is *much* easier to use than brushes and rollers. It also dries faster. Ask your public works department or local paint store to recommend outdoor spray paints that will last when exposed to weather and foot traffic.

Prepare to Spray

It's best to stencil with two friends. If a grown-up can come along, that's OK, too. Never stencil alone. The pavement should be dry, the day calm, and the temperature above 50 degrees. Wind and rain will ruin a stenciling day. Place the safety cones on either side of the storm drain. One person should stand on the sidewalk to watch for cars and answer questions from onlookers. Use your wire brush to clean the sidewalk pavement directly above the drain (or wherever the stencil is most appropriate), and put any garbage you collect in a trash bag. You should clean a rectangular area about 1.5 feet by 2.5 feet. If cars are parked closer than 10 feet, wait to spray until they have been moved.

Two coats of paint are best: one background color (white), and one message color (blue or green). Lay background stencil on the pavement, align properly, and tape down corners. Read the instructions on the spray can before spraying. Don't spray too much or the paint will flow under the stencil. Let it dry. Lay the message stencil over the painted background rectangle, and tape down the corners. Spray again. Collect your kit and move on. If you have a lot of drains to stencil, you can spray all of the backgrounds first, then circle back and spray the messages.

If you want to practice your spraying before you hit the streets, do so on top of some scrap wood or old newspapers taped to the pavement.

Clean Up

After each time you spray, wipe off excess paint from the stencil with some towels or rags. While walking between drains, carry your stencils in a trash bag so you don't get paint on anything.

Watch

Now that you have your local storm drains identified and stenciled, make it a habit to walk by them on a regular basis to look for illegal dumping and to check the status of your storm drain stencil. If you spot someone dumping waste down a storm drain, telephone your city's public works department.

Educate

If there are houses near your adopted storm drains, drop off a one-page information sheet about storm drain pollution. You can write it yourself by using the information you learned from this book or the Greenpatch Gang comic *The Case of the Contaminated Canine*. Let your neighbors know what not to put down the storm drain and how to prevent water pollution. Once they learn, they'll become storm drain watchers, too!

Testing the Waters

Here are some simple ways you can detect pollutants flowing along your gutters, down your storm drains, and into a nearby waterway.

Look and Smell

The first thing you should always do is look at the water. Simple observation is an important scientific tool, and it is sometimes an easy way for you to detect the results of illegal dumping or accidental spills. In addition to the specific pollutants listed below, always look for paper, plastic, and other garbage. Also, watch for weird colors in the water. And remember, if the water looks strange, don't touch it.

Oil and Gas. Oil and gas have a distinct petroleum smell. Other wastes have a variety of unnatural smells that will warn you of pollution. When oil and gas are dumped into water, they tend to float on the surface. Oil "globs" together and makes the water's surface shiny and off-colored. Gas spreads out evenly and produces a shiny, multicolored surface.

Silt. Excessive soil erosion is also considered pollution. Muddy-looking water loaded with silt can harm aquatic plants and animals downstream. Silt is also a sign that harmful erosion is occurring upstream.

Soap. When soap hits water, it forms bubbles or foam. Soaps and cleaners that don't form bubbles can usually be detected with a pH test strip.

Antifreeze. Large quantities of antifreeze make water look green; smaller amounts make water look milky.

Paint. Paint is one of the most common products dumped down storm drains. If the water is colored and not by antifreeze, paint could be the culprit.

Sample and Test

If the water you're watching doesn't look shiny, milky, colored, muddy, or foamy, and it doesn't smell bad, but you are still suspicious, take a sample. There are two simple tests you can conduct with your water sample.

What you need:
rubber gloves
clean plastic bottle with tight-fitting lid
pH aquatic test strips
microscope

1. Put on your gloves and fill your bottle at the water's surface. Use the buddy system, and make sure a grown-up knows where you are. Also, if you're by a natural waterway, pick a safe spot (without steep banks or fast water) to collect your sample so you won't fall in.
2. Be careful handling your sample at all times.
3. When you're done collecting and testing, remove your gloves and wash your hands.
4. If you see a suspicious spill or weird waste entering a storm drain near an industrial area, **don't collect a sample**. Contact your public works department or toxic spill hotline.

pH Aquatic Test Strips

After you collect a water sample from the gutter or from a nearby waterway, dip a pH test strip into your sample. Read the instructions from the test strip kit for how long to soak it. The strip might turn a color, either pink or blue. Place it alongside the colored and numbered chart from the kit. A result below 5 is acidic (pink). A result above 8 is basic (blue). A result between 5 and 8 is neutral (no color change). Many pollutants show up either as acidic or basic on these strips. Normal fresh water is neutral.

Although the results of a pH test can give you clues about what pollutants you

Blue. This could mean some type of soap, detergent, fertilizer, or ammonia has polluted the water.

Pink. This could mean that acid from a car battery has polluted the water. If it has rained recently, it could also indicate that air pollution from automobiles and industry polluted the rainwater, creating "acid rain."

might have found, the only way to positively identify specific pollutants is to have a professional lab test the water. If you are suspicious, tell your public works department about your results.

Look at water samples taken from a waterway (*not* gutters) with a microscope. You can tell if the water is healthy. This is basically a counting game. Place a drop of water from your sample on a glass slide and put it under the microscope.

Healthy fresh water should have a reasonable population of wiggling microorganisms (favorite foods for fish). However, if your water drop is packed with microorganisms, it could mean that too many nutrients are in the water, most likely from sewage. If there are *no* microorganisms in your sample, it is not good news. They might have been killed by pollution. Without microorganisms, there can be no fish, frogs, turtles, or other aquatic species.

volvocids

diatoms

Numerous microorganisms live in fresh water, such as the two shown above.

Storm Drain Pollutants

Storm Drain Pollutants	Alternatives
Oil-based paints, turpentine, thinners	Water-based latex paints
Stains and finishes	Latex paint or natural earth pigment finishes
Paint strippers	Sandpaper, heat gun
Sulfur-based fungicides	Don't overwater garden, and keep it clean and dry. Use less toxic fungicides.
Weed killers	Pull weeds *before* they flower, and compost them.
Chemical fertilizers	Use compost or organic soil amendments: peat moss, blood meal, bone meal, fish emulsion, manure, seaweed.
Roach, ant, and rodent poisons	Remove food supply, plug entry points, and use traps.
Garden insecticides	Keep your garden clean. Buy predators: ladybugs and praying mantises. Use insecticidal soap and insect traps.
Plastic	Limit your use of plastic. Dispose of it properly. Take recyclable plastic to a recycling center.

Where to Buy pH Aquatic Test Strips

Scientific supply stores carry test strip kits. You can order by telephone or mail from Edmund Scientific. Another excellent source is a pool supplies company, or the pool supplies section of your local hardware store. For under $10, you can buy a box of about 50 strips that come with a color-coded and numbered chart to help you interpret your test results.

Write, or telephone: Edmund Scientific Company, 101 E. Gloucester Pike, Barrington, NJ 08007-1380, 609-573-6250.

What to Do with Wastes

Used motor oil, antifreeze, pesticides, herbicides, oil-based paints, gasoline, paint thinner, turpentine: Place in a sturdy, sealed container, tape cap on, label with a permanent ink marker, and ask your local recyclers where you can drop it off or if they will pick it up.

Chlorinated water from swimming pools and hot tubs: Before draining, let water stand for two weeks so the chlorine can evaporate. Don't add more chlorine to the water during this period.

Latex paints: Air dry in can, and discard in trash can. Don't pour clean-up water down storm drains.

Greenpatch Kids

Watershed Watchers

When Ellen Hayes started teaching her sixth-grade science students at Western Heights Middle School about biodiversity and watersheds, she had no idea they would end up teaching *her* something. "We took the students to our outdoor school for a day," explains teacher Hayes, "and started talking about watersheds. The kids came up to me and said, 'Your ideas are really neat, but let's narrow this down. Let's look at what *our* watershed is doing to Chesapeake Bay.'"

Western Heights Middle School is located in Hagerstown, Maryland, on the northeastern slope of the Appalachian Mountains. Water passing through Hagerstown's watershed winds its way some 80 miles eastward before entering Chesapeake Bay. "The city built a runoff holding pond on the school property a couple of years ago," says Hayes, "so the kids said, 'Hey, we've got this ugly pond here, maybe we could turn that into a wetland as part of our watershed study.' So we said, 'Well, you can try.'"

"We wanted to give something back to the community and to all the animals that live around here," explains Jasen Logsdon, who was in the first class of sixth graders to work on the project. "So we began to build the wetlands around the pond. The teachers gave us books and magazines to study, then we decided what plants to buy and put in the ground. We did this to create a buffer around the pond, so when the rains come, there won't be erosion. Also, the kids down in woodshop built birdhouses to put around the pond."

The kids also have water-testing equipment to monitor the conditions of their watershed. "We learned how to test the water quality," Jasen explains. "When it rains, the water stays in our pond where we are building the wetlands. Well, we tested that water. Then we traced the water from the top of our watershed. We went to Tom's Run, the Conococheague Creek, and the Potomac River, and took samples and brought them back to our school. We tested for pH, nitrates, temperature, oxygen content, and to see if the water was cloudy or colored. We also added different chemicals and watched what happened. Depending on what color the water turned, we could tell what

might be in it. There are all sorts of test kits we used to look for different things. We also used microscopes. We learned a lot about chemistry, biology, and all sorts of things."

Classmate Jadah Zampelli details another part of her school's efforts. "We started a storm drain stenciling project to teach people that polluting the environment could affect people in the year 2000. The stencil says, 'Don't Dump—Chesapeake Bay Drainage.' If we don't do projects like these, people in the next century may not have a Chesapeake Bay like the one we know now— it might be polluted if we don't take care of the water. There is no question that if you throw a piece of garbage, or anything, into the water here it will end up in the Chesapeake."

The students at Western Heights Middle School hope to continue their water-testing studies, wetlands creation, and planting project for years to come. "I used to think, 'Hey, what if I just threw one piece of trash in the water, it won't make a difference,'" says Jadah. "But you learn what a difference one piece of trash can make. By working on this project I learned how I could make a difference and help save Chesapeake Bay."

The Water Planet

Without water, there would be no life on Earth as we know it. In fact, the first living organisms (many of which were bacteria) evolved in Earth's oceans billions of years ago. *All* living things are made of water. Your body, for example, is 60 percent water. Water helps clean the inside of you (blood is about 50 percent water) and the outside of you. Water gives life to everything.

A Finite Resource

Water is a finite resource. That is, there is a fixed amount of water on the planet, and no new water is ever going to be produced. Earth is sometimes called the Water Planet because about 70 percent of its surface is covered by oceans. Oceans hold about 98 percent of Earth's water. Only about 2 percent of Earth's water is fresh. Of that 2 percent, 75 percent is stored in glaciers at the North and South Poles. The rest is stored as groundwater, in rivers and lakes, as moisture in the soil, and in the *atmosphere* (the envelope of air that surrounds Earth).

What Goes Around Comes Around

If most of Earth's water is salty, how come our drinking water isn't salty? Thanks to Earth's amazing water cycle, we get fresh water from the oceans. Here's how. Solar energy heats the surface of the ocean and causes water molecules to *evaporate*. They detach from the surface of the ocean and enter the air as water vapor, a gas. When evaporation takes place, minerals and salts are left behind.

The vapor rises into the atmosphere. As it rises, it cools. When it reaches its *dew point* (the temperature at which water molecules come together to make water droplets), clouds are formed.

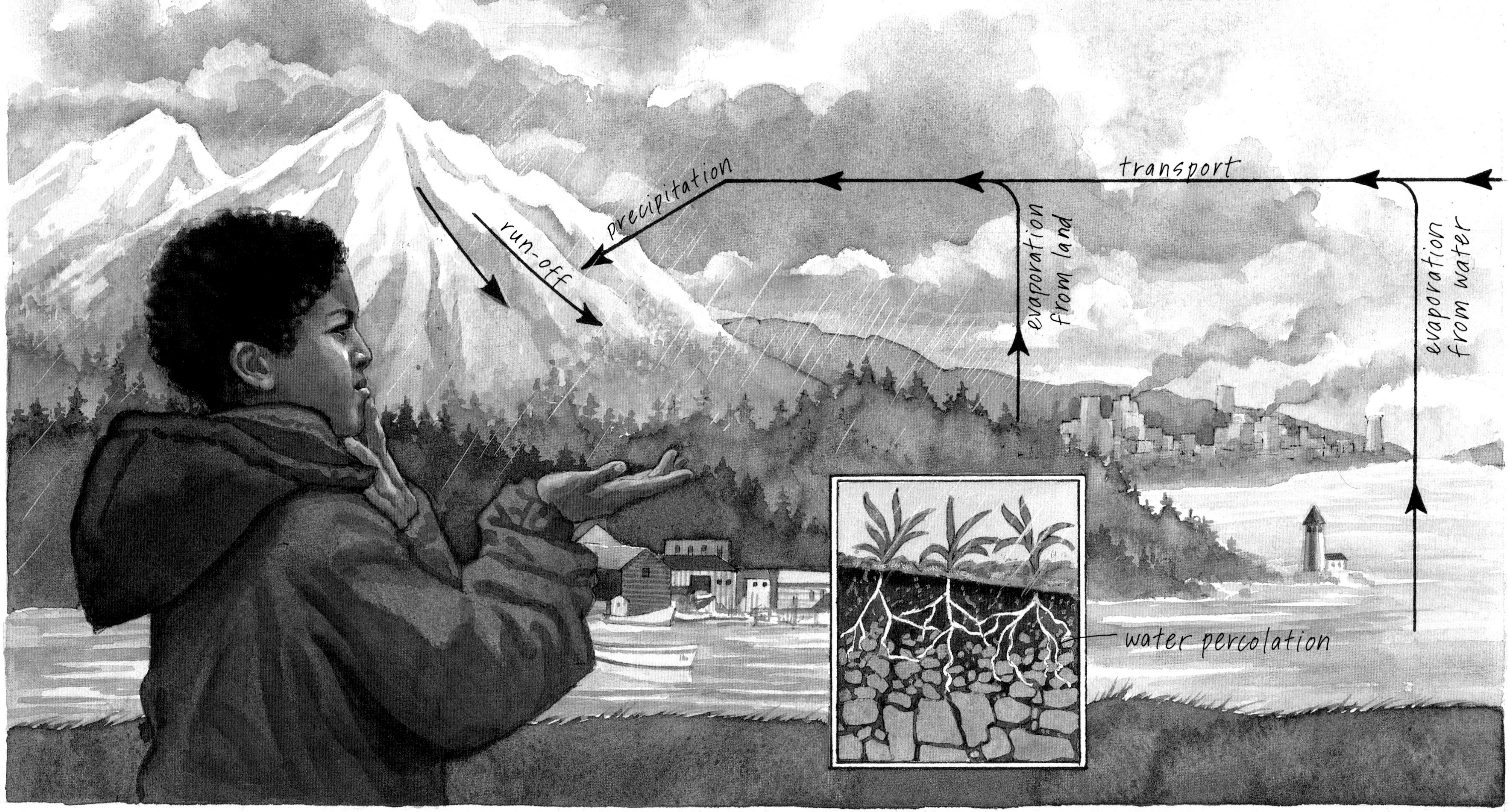

evaporation from water

water percolation

transport

evaporation from land

precipitation

run-off

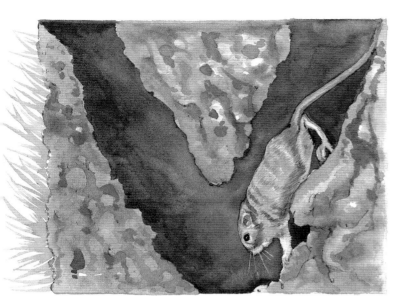

Water on the Move

The airborne water then begins to move around the planet. Trade winds over the oceans move moist air toward the equator, where it's warmed, rises, cools, and falls as rain. Equatorial areas are the wettest on Earth. The air that rises over the equator descends in two subtropical zones, around 30 degrees north and south of the equator. As this air descends, it warms, and a little rain falls. A portion of this air returns toward the equator (picking up more moisture) and is recycled. The rest moves toward the poles. Between 30 and 60 degrees north and south, rain is common. Here, air rises again because it's either heated over warm land or it's forced upward by a wedge of cold polar air. In the freezing polar regions, the high-altitude air descends again, and it is dry. (Did you know that only about 4 inches of snow falls each year at the North Pole? That is less precipitation than in some desert areas. But it's so cold, there is *no* evaporation.)

Got it? This means that the molecules of water that fell on your head during the last rainstorm might have once been on the back of a sea turtle surfacing for air off Cuba, and may have been part of the Amazon River before that!

When water reaches the earth as rain, some of it soaks into the soil and is stored as groundwater. People will use some of it, but most eventually makes its way back to the oceans via streams and rivers. When it enters the ocean, the water cycle starts all over again.

[Diagram labels: air descending, air rising, surface winds, equator, global circulation, 60° N., 30° N., 0°, 30° S., 60° S.]

Virga

Question: What's it called when it rains, but the raindrops evaporate before they reach the ground? Answer: *Virga.* Virga is common in hot areas of the world, such as deserts and inland plains. The next time you visit one of these places, look for a wispy curtain of rain with a tattered bottom edge floating above the land. It's beautiful.

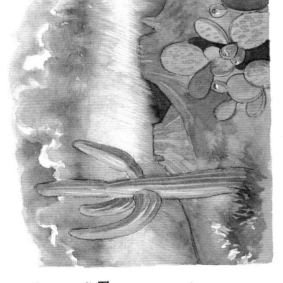

Be Water Wise

Do you know where your drinking water comes from? Call up your local water company (or ask at city hall), and then go on a tour of the closest water distribution plant. You might be surprised how far your water has to travel before it gets into your glass.

It doesn't matter if you live in the desert, the humid East Coast, or the rainy Northwest, and it doesn't matter if you get your water from a well or from a municipal system: *Saving water around the house is important.*

Fix leaks. One leaky faucet can waste up to 25,000 gallons a year! Don't let water run. Turn it off while you're brushing your teeth or doing the dishes. Install a low-flow shower head. Don't overwater lawns. Use drip irrigation in the garden.

About *half* of all the water you use goes down the toilet. Old toilets use between 5 and 7 gallons per flush. New toilets (which work just as well as the old ones) only use 1.6 gallons per flush—a big difference! Some water companies will even help you buy new toilets because they save so much water.

If you have a pool, keep it covered when not in use.

Disappearing Act

Sometimes evaporation is hard to understand. When you hang up wet clothes outside to dry, where does all that water go? Here is how you can get a good feel for evaporation in your own room.

What you need:
black ink marker
small glass
water
saucer
glass bowl

1. Draw a line about halfway up the small glass.
2. Fill the glass with water to the line.
3. Now pour the water from the glass into the saucer.
4. Refill the glass to the line.
5. Cover the glass with the bowl.
6. Leave both the saucer and the covered glass in a warm place. Come back after a few hours. What happened?

---

much body liquid through evaporation. They live in burrows deep in the cool ground. When they leave or enter their burrow, they plug the hole to keep moisture inside. They don't urinate a lot, and the urine they do expel is concentrated. Where do they get water? Kangaroo rats save so much water in their bodies, they can get all the water they need from a bit of vegetation and seeds, even though seeds are only 4 percent water! Now *that* is true water conservation.

Animals That Never Drink Water

Some desert animals—especially rodents—never drink water. Here is how kangaroo rats survive: They are only active at night when it's cooler, so they don't lose

Catch That Toilet

Is your toilet running? Then catch it. Slow, quiet toilet leaks waste up to 40 gallons of water a day.

What you need:
bottle of blue food coloring (or dye tablet from your water company)
watch

1. Take the lid off the toilet tank.
2. Put in about ten drops of the food coloring, or one of the dye tablets.

3. Take note of the time on your watch, and wait five minutes. When the time is up, look at the water in the toilet bowl. If it's clear, then your toilet isn't running. If it's blue, you have a leak.

Toilet leaks mean either the float ball in the tank is set too high, or the rubber stopper and valve seat at the bottom of the tank are worn and cracked. If you find a leak, have a grown-up help you inspect the float ball, stopper, and valve.

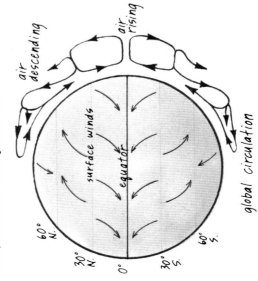

Great Green Recyclers

Some of the most important water recyclers are growing all around you. Plants recycle water by absorbing it from the soil and releasing it as water vapor into the atmosphere. In parts of the world with dense vegetation, such as tropical rain forests, plants produce so much water vapor that clouds and rain are almost always in the sky.

Plants help our soil, air, and climates stay healthy. They also helped humans evolve. Millions of years ago, when the atmosphere was full of deadly gases, small green plants produced our oxygen-packed atmosphere. Through *photosynthesis*, marine algae in the ancient oceans helped create the atmosphere we now have. Today, all plants help our atmosphere stay healthy by constantly absorbing carbon dioxide gas and producing oxygen.

Making Their Own Food

The term photosynthesis comes from the Greek words meaning "light" and "to put together." Using a special chemical called chlorophyll, plants store the energy of sunlight. This stored energy makes carbohydrates from carbon dioxide and water. (Carbohydrates are important sources of nourishment for all living things.) Plants use carbohydrates for energy and to synthesize proteins, fats, and other vital chemicals.

The Downside of Leaves

The underside of each plant leaf is covered by small holes called *stomata*. When sunlight reaches plants, photosynthesis takes place. The stomata open so carbon dioxide can enter and oxygen and water vapor can leave. This production of water vapor is called *transpiration*. If a plant needs water but the day is hot, the stomata close to conserve water.

For plants, oxygen is a waste product they must get rid of in order to survive. That is

Plant Life Cycles

Annual plants (plants that live only one growing season) age rapidly and die after they flower and produce seeds. Their cells have a limited ability to reproduce and stay alive. *Perennial* plants (plants that live longer than one growing season) live for many years. Some trees live for hundreds or even thousands of years, always continuing to grow. They get around the problems of aging and early death by forming large numbers of new cells each year while equal numbers of old cells die.

California's giant sequoias are some of the oldest living things on Earth. Some are more than 4,000 years old and over 300 feet tall. But these ancient trees contain no living cells that are any older than you are. If their cells didn't constantly age and die, and if new cells weren't produced, the trees would never last 4,000 years.

new cells
dead cells

convenient for us oxygen-breathing animals. Plants *inhale* what you exhale as waste from your lungs—carbon dioxide—and they *exhale* what you need to inhale and live—oxygen.

Hairy Roots, Dude

When you look at a plant, you are only seeing part of it. The other part is underground, and it is mostly roots. There are many forms of roots. Some grow deep into the soil. Others spread sideways.

Regardless of shape, all roots are covered by millions of tiny hairs to help the plant find water and minerals. Some plants have billions of hairs on their root system. If the roots and root hairs of one of these plants were combined into a single root, it would be hundreds of miles long.

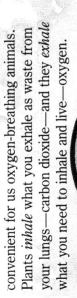

Greenpatch Alert:
Endangered Plants

Many plants are endangered due to habitat destruction. Be careful what plants you snip, clip, and grow. If you would like to find out more about endangered plants and what you can do to help them, contact your local native plant society or your state's fish and game department.

For information about federally endangered plant species, write to: U.S. Fish and Wildlife Service, Division of Endangered Species, 4401 North Fairfax Drive, MS-452-ARLSQ, Arlington, VA 22203. No self-addressed, stamped envelope is necessary.

Blue Celery

Water moves up through a plant from cell to cell through a process called *osmosis*. To help you see osmosis in action, that piece of celery in your refrigerator will do just fine.

What you need:
glass jar
water
blue food coloring
stick of celery
knife

1. Fill the glass jar halfway with water.
2. Add five drops of blue food coloring.
3. Make a clean cut across the bottom of the celery stick (the widest end), and place that end in the water.
4. Place the jar and the celery on a counter and check it every few hours. How long does it take for the celery to turn blue?

Next time you find a rubbery piece of celery in the bottom of your refrigerator, give it a drink. Cut the bottom end, and place it in water. What happens?

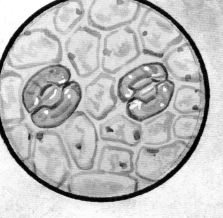

17

Death in the Forest

The old raccoon lived a long life—13 years, in fact. He was born inside a towering cottonwood, near a sandy bend on a river. It was an ideal home for a raccoon family. The enormous tree provided warmth in winter and cool interiors during summer heat. Along the riverbank, crayfish, snails, and stranded fish made easy meals. Inland, worms, bird eggs, corn patches, and scraps from backyard dog bowls were abundant.

His parents forced him out of the den one day, so he set off by himself. Years later, he settled in the river's wooded headwaters, some 30 miles from his birthplace. During his lifetime he knew many female raccoons and started many families. But on a warm spring night when a strong young male invaded his territory, there was a fight. The old male lost. He was badly bitten around his neck, and his right shoulder was torn open.

An hour after his fight, the old raccoon lay down on the forest floor, slowly bleeding to death. Two hours later, as a gentle wind moved across the surrounding pines and the birch leaves danced in the moonlight, he stopped breathing.

In the half-light of dawn, a passing bobcat made a quick meal of the raccoon. The bobcat ate part of the raccoon's exposed shoulder, chewed part of his rib cage, and left the rest. By midmorning, ants were searching the carcass for moisture and minerals, and a rowdy group of ravens touched down for a meal. The ravens were followed by two circling turkey vultures, and soon they, too, were tugging at the carcass. In the afternoon heat,

bluebottle flies laid eggs inside the ripening carcass, and yellow jackets cut off chunks of raccoon meat with their powerful jaws. Bacteria and fungi were spreading quickly across the body.

· Within several days, much of the carcass was gone. Carrion beetles dug under the smelly remains to lay eggs. The beetle and fly eggs soon hatched into hundreds of flesh-eating maggots.

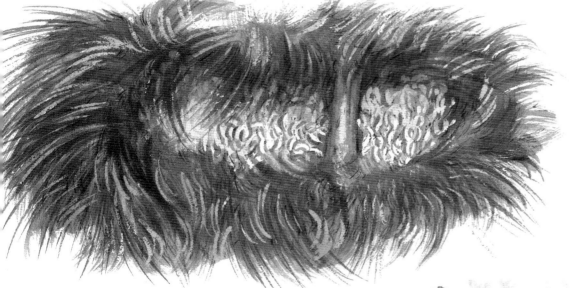

What's That Smell?

The very things that help animals (and people) live also cause them to rot and stink when they die. Intestinal bacteria, stomach acids, and enzymes help live animals digest their food. When an animal dies, these things keep on digesting, but now they eat away at the dead body from inside.

Intestinal bacteria create foul-smelling gas as they decompose the rotting body. This putrid gas also causes some dead animals to bloat (inflate like a balloon). The gas combines with rotting body parts and decayed blood to form two chemicals that add to the smell: *putrescine* and *cadaverine*.

Two weeks after his last fight, all that was left of the old raccoon was a scattering of bones, hair, and bits of dried skin.

Scavenger Avengers

Perhaps the most visible scavenger—and to some the ugliest—is the vulture. Who would want to eat rotting animals, anyway? There are three species of vultures in North America: black vulture, turkey vulture, and California condor. All belong to the family *Cathartidae*, from a Greek word meaning "cleanser." And cleanse they do.

Vultures are perfectly adapted to eat *carrion* (dead, rotting flesh). Their excellent eyesight and keen sense of smell enable vultures to find carcasses from far away. Their heads are featherless. When they finish a meal of carrion, any infectious bacteria they might have picked up are exposed to sunlight and not given a chance to grow under their feathers. Their digestive systems are equipped with strong acids and enzymes to kill infectious bacteria they swallow.

Vultures, and most other scavengers, have a bad reputation because they are misunderstood. But without them our environment would be a lot less healthy, and a lot stinkier.

Flattened Fauna

Question: Why did the prairie chicken cross the road? Answer: It didn't, because it got smashed by a speeding car. Roads are unnatural habitats for animals, but animals still have to cross roads or fly over them to get to the other side. Some animals use roads as trails because they are open and easy to move on; others lie down on them for warmth. Scavengers search out roadkills for food, and sometimes become roadkills themselves.

There is a seasonality to roadkills that will become obvious to you if you start a hit list. In the spring, frogs, toads, and salamanders cross roads during migration. In the summer, many baby mammals linger at roadsides because they haven't yet learned to fear cars.

During the fall, when temperatures begin to drop, snakes slither onto roads because roads retain warmth. Fall is also the peak time for skunks as they wander about during their breeding season. Early winter and late spring is a time when young, low-flying owls pass over roads. Where ancient migration routes cross roads, or where a habitat has been sliced in two by pavement, there can be dozens of roadkills. In some of these areas, special tunnels have been built so animals can pass unharmed. In California's Tilden Park, a road is closed from October through April so thousands of California newts can cross the road to their breeding ponds.

Cowabunga! Cow Pie

What is waste to one animal is food for another. Cow pies and other piles of *dung* (animal feces) are favorite foods and egg-laying sites for many flies, beetles, and worms.

Dung beetles, tumblebugs, and flies lay eggs in and under cow dung. Their larvae hatch and eat their way through the dung. Earthworms congregate underneath, and fungi soon sprout on top. Within a week, the dung piles can completely disappear!

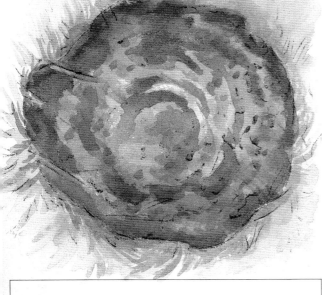

Make a Hit List

It is always fun and interesting to watch for live wildlife while on road trips, but flattened roadside fauna can also tell you a lot about the seasons and the country you're driving through. Here is how you can turn your road trips into zoological expeditions.

What you need:

notebook
pen or pencil
keen eyes

1. Open your notebook and draw five columns on the page. Number the lines down the first column. Write *Date* at the top of the second column, *Species Name* on the third, *Location* (highway number) on the fourth, and *Condition* (fresh, old, bits and pieces) on the fifth.

2. Keep a hit list for a year. By studying it you will learn what animals are most active, when, and where.

Greenpatch Alert:
Endangered Scavenger California Condor

When North America knew the scream of saber-toothed tigers and felt the weight of giant ground sloths, mastodons, camels, and other huge animals (all known as *megafauna*), thousands of condors rode the winds with wings that stretched almost 10 feet across.

Today, the condor population numbers less than 100.

What happened to this magnificent bird? Scientists aren't completely sure, but they know that after the extinction of North America's megafauna, the decrease in grazing animal populations, and the increase in humans, the condor's food source and habitat began to disappear. By 1900, most con-

dors had retreated to the rugged mountains of southern California.

During the 1940s, the condor's habitat was sprayed with the pesticide DDT to kill harmful crop insects, and poison was used to kill ground squirrels on grazing lands. By eating animals that died from these poisons, the condor population weakened. Also, California's human population skyrocketed after World War II and intruded on feeding areas.

By 1982, less than 25 condors remained. But a captive breeding program operated by the federal government has been successful. Today, 6 released condors survive in their former habitat. More releases are planned in the future. With a decrease in the use of harmful pesticides throughout the con-

dor's former range, and education of the public, condor experts are hopeful these graceful birds will once again roam the skies over parts of North America.

To find out more about California condors and what you can do to help them, write: U.S. Fish and Wildlife Service, California Condor Recovery Program, P.O. Box 5839, Ventura, CA 93005. No self-addressed, stamped envelope is necessary.

The Bone Yard

Animal skeletons and bone fragments can be found everywhere, even in your backyard. Start a bone yard by collecting weathered skeletons and bones (the ones that are white and free of animal pieces). To find out which animal owned those bones, look for *The Audubon Society Field Guide to Mammals* by John O. Whitaker, New York: Alfred A. Knopf, 1980, or *A Field Guide to the Mammals* by William Burt and Richard Grossenheider, Boston: Houghton Mifflin, 1976.

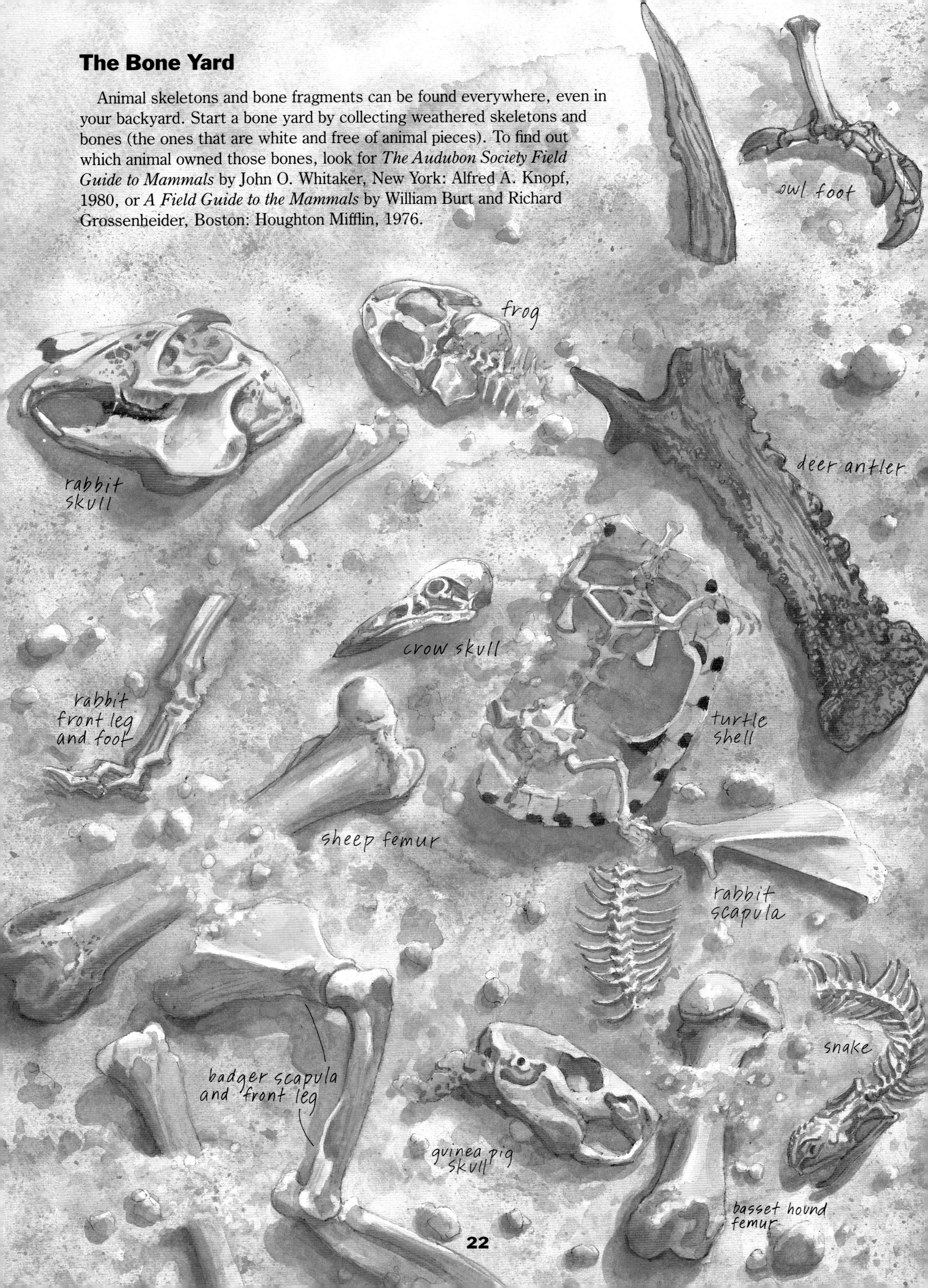

owl foot

frog

deer antler

rabbit skull

crow skull

turtle shell

rabbit front leg and foot

sheep femur

rabbit scapula

badger scapula and front leg

snake

guinea pig skull

basset hound femur

22

Them Clean Bones

The collection and study of skeletons and single bones can teach you how animals are built and help you identify other specimens that you find. Universities and museums have large colonies of dermestid beetles that clean the bones of dead animals in a couple of weeks. (Look in Resources to find out where to buy your own dermestids.)

However, scientists sometimes skin and boil the carcasses before giving them to the dermestids! If you don't want to do that, here is an easier way to clean the skeletons of dead animals you have found.

What you need:
small dead animal (mouse or bird)
gloves
shovel or trowel
large rock or brick
old clay plant pot
stick
water
bleach

1. Never kill an animal just for its skeleton. Use only dead animals that you've found.

2. When you find the carcass of a small animal, put on your gloves, pick it up, and carry it to a remote corner of your yard.

3. Dig a shallow pit, place the carcass inside, and cover with dirt.

4. Place the large rock or brick on top of the dirt, directly above the carcass, so other animals won't dig it up.

5. Take your stick and poke it in the ground near the rock to mark the spot.

6. Wait a few months, then dig it up. If there is still some flesh remaining on the animal, rebury it for another month or two.

Another method is to lay your carcass on the open ground in a remote corner and place your pot on top of it, upside down. Make sure there is space around the edges of the pot for ants and beetles to enter. This way you can check the process every now and again by lifting the pot. The solid bones of mammals clean up best. Bird bones are hollow, and sometimes fall apart, but their skulls and beaks almost always stay in one piece.

When the carcass is cleaned and dry, put your gloves on, and scrape off any remaining dried bits of flesh with a stick. Place the bones in a bucket containing a mixture of water and bleach for a few minutes. Remove and rinse thoroughly with fresh water. Dry them in the sun. They are now ready to be labeled and added to your collection.

Warning: Bleach can be harmful if not used properly. Ask a grown-up to help you with the water-and-bleach mixture. If you find a carcass that is squashed beyond recognition, or covered with flies and maggots, or smelly, *don't collect it!* Wait until you find a complete carcass that is a bit "fresher."

Greenpatch Kid

Bone Collector

Jaime Merritt's bedroom is really a bone room. Dozens of animal skulls line the top of his bookcase, and other bones are scattered about here and there. "I've always been interested in biology," says Jaime, who has been collecting and cleaning bones since he was ten years old. "Preparing bones teaches you a lot about anatomy and how animals work. You get to look at how the bones move and how the animal is put together. You learn a lot."

Jaime uses several techniques to prepare bones. One of the procedures uses dermestid beetles to clean up animals that Jaime has found. These are the same type of beetles that help decompose animals when they die outdoors. "I bought some dermestid beetles and started going at it," explains Jaime. "I had my own beetle colony in my basement for a long time.

I had them in two 5-gallon ice cream containers, and they never smelled up the basement. If I didn't have an animal that I was working on, I would give the beetles a piece of dried chicken. But if I was working on an animal, I would let it dry out and give it to the beetles and let them eat it."

Jaime explains that when you prepare a skeleton with most other methods, such as boiling or with chemicals, you end up with a pile of disorganized bones. But not so with dermestid beetles. "With dermestids," explains Jaime, "you come out with almost a complete skeleton because they don't eat the cartilage between the bones. You just have to strengthen some of the joints. To reconstruct bones, you use a strong, waterproof, fast-drying glue. If a few bones have come apart, you have to use something, like clay or wire, to hold them together."

The biggest animal Jaime has ever worked on was a fox. "And," he adds, "I have most of a deer that I found outdoors. The smallest? I have a frog skeleton. And I still have a bunch of animals in plastic bags in our basement freezer."

Jaime has some tips for collecting dead animals. "Always carry a good pair of latex gloves and large plastic garbage bags in your car. And always look for traffic when you stop. Don't touch the animal with your bare hands, because it's not going to be that clean. The best place to look for animals is on country roads that get some traffic, but not too much. And don't stop for something unless it looks *really* good. If the animal is smooshed, forget it." Jaime also suggests that if you're going to put dead animals in the freezer for storage, they should be placed in airtight plastic bags and clearly labeled. Also, don't forget to ask permission before you store a carcass in the freezer.

Down on the Floor

The forest floor where the old raccoon died might look calm and silent, but it's really a very active place. Instead of just walking through the woods looking at the trees, or strolling in the nearby park the next time you're on a hike, get down on the ground on all fours (your hands and knees) and poke around. You'll discover that eating, digestion, waste production, and decomposition are taking place right under your feet all the time. When an animal dies, or a leaf falls to the soil, or a tree topples over, decomposition creatures arrive for a meal, and microscopic bacteria and fungi begin their work.

Decomposition Creatures

Decomposition creatures live inside and on top of the soil. They help break down everything, small bite by small bite, from dead raccoons to tree trunks. They're also fun to watch.

Here are some of the most common decomposition creatures. But keep your eyes open. You'll see a lot more. Also, larger animals in search of food will be attracted to soil that's home to decomposition creatures. Watch for signs of worm-loving moles burrowing underground, quick-tongued lizards skittering after a meal, and birds doing the soil shuffle as they scratch for a snack. At night, skunks, raccoons, foxes, and opossums sniff and rummage about searching for worms and other creatures.

Sow Bugs and Pill Bugs

These two pea-sized cousins are not insects at all, but small crustaceans with segmented shells. They are related to lobsters, crabs, and crayfish. You will probably find both of these armored gray dynamos living underneath fallen leaves and rotting logs. They both eat plant material.

If you poke a pill bug, it will roll into a ball. If you poke a sow bug, it won't roll into a ball. Although these crustaceans are great decomposers, they also munch young seedlings. If you see them around your garden, it's best to move them. (Don't worry, they don't bite.)

Earwigs

No, earwigs won't crawl into your ear at night and eat your brain, as people once thought they did. Earwigs are brown and under 1 inch long. Although they have short leathery wings, they almost always crawl. Their main interest is decaying organic material, like plants. That's why the underside of a leaf pile sometimes looks like an earwig party. They may not crawl into your ear, but those rear-end pinchers really work, so watch out.

Earthworms

Earthworms may be the most visible soil dwellers. These master tunnelers eat their way through the soil with the help of strong muscles and small bristles that cover their slimy bodies. As they burrow around, they swallow scraps, microorganisms, soil, and everything else. With the help of bacteria that live in their gut, earthworms digest all this material and leave behind a trail of nutrient-packed droppings called *castings*. With their constant burrowing and creation of castings, earthworms help improve the soil.

Earthworms are *hermaphrodites* (have both male and female sexual organs) and can begin reproducing when they are only three months old. If you dig around, you may find worms that are stuck to each other along one side of their bodies. That's a mating pair.

Both worms will produce one ¼-inch egg (the size of a kernel of corn) a week after mating. In three weeks, between one and five baby worms will emerge from each egg.

Beetles

A wide variety of ground beetles (also called caterpillar beetles) live close to decomposing things because they eat decomposition creatures. Most of these beetles are about 1 inch long and are black or dark green. They hide under the edges of rotting things during the day and come out at night to hunt.

Several beetle species, such as the fiery searcher, darkling beetle, and bombardier beetle, are sometimes called stink beetles because they will squirt you with a smelly secretion from their rear end if you pick one up. Ground beetles eat decomposition creatures, but beetle droppings help enrich the soil.

Nematodes

Nematodes look simple and slimy, but these small clear worms have digestive systems, nervous systems, and several different muscles (a magnifying glass might help you see them better). Nematodes are mostly *parasites* (they live on or in other living species), but they also consume anything that is rotting.

There are an estimated 500,000 species of nematodes in the world, ranging in size from microscopic species on the ocean floor to 20-foot-long species living inside whales. There are also species that live on the forest floor. Grab a lens, uncover a moist bunch of rotting leaves, and see if you can find them.

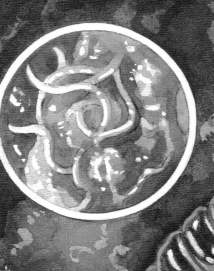

Springtails

Springtails are small, wingless, ftealike insects that are found in soil everywhere. They are called springtails because when disturbed they use a lever under their stomachs to catapult themselves into the air. Is your soil hopping? Maybe you have an outbreak of springtails.

Springtails chew on soft plant materials and occasionally on nematodes.

Centipedes

The centipede, or "100-legger," is really the "40-to-50-legger," depending on the species. Centipedes (and millipedes) are not true insects but relatives of scorpions and spiders. Much like ground beetles, centipedes are beneficial garden predators. Centipedes feed at night on soil insects and millipedes. Like beetles, their droppings help improve the soil.

Millipedes

The millipede, or "1,000-legger," doesn't really have that many legs, it just looks as if it does. Adult millipedes have closer to 200 pairs of legs. When these wavy-legged creatures are disturbed, they roll up into a ball.

Millipedes frequent piles of rotting things because they eat decaying plants. Like the sow and pill bugs, millipedes can sometimes devour your young seedlings, so it's a good idea to keep them out of the newly planted vegetable patch.

25

Big-Time Decomposers

In Praise of Bacteria

Bacteria are the key to *all* decomposition. Bacteria help you—and all other species and ecosystems—survive. Without bacteria, all living things would die, because they wouldn't be able to digest food. Without bacteria, life as you know it wouldn't exist.

Bacteria are single-celled organisms that live everywhere. They can be found high above the ground or in the depths of the ocean; from the outer layers of you to inside your intestines; from earthworm guts to soil everywhere.

Bacteria are so small that about 1,000 average-sized bacteria can fit on the head of a pin. Most bacteria move with the help of *flagella* (hairlike whips), and when they want to reproduce, they simply divide into two exactly equal bacteria. These amazing organisms don't have mouths or stomachs, so they absorb nutrients directly through their cell wall. Bacteria enzymes help break down nutrients, and this is how bacteria survive.

Countless types of bacteria live in soil. There they biodegrade organic materials and help plants grow. Bacteria also live *inside* decomposition creatures, and all animals, to help them absorb hard-to-digest stuff.

The Fungus Among Us

Mushrooms and other fungi are also important decomposers and digesters of the forest floor. Mushrooms survive three different ways. Some are *parasitic*, feeding on the living tissues of their host plant or animal. Others are *saprophytic*, feeding on the decomposing material of dead plants and animals. Yet others develop *symbiotic relationships*, feeding on living plants while also helping to feed those plants.

As mushrooms grow, they produce a mass of fuzzy threadlike strands called *mycelia*. Mycelia either spread out and tap into the living cells of plants and animals (parasitic fungi), wrap around dead plant and animal material (saprophytic fungi), or grow alongside the roots of living plants (symbiotic fungi). Although all three types of mushrooms are decomposers, saprophytic mushrooms are the master decomposers. Their mycelia produce digestive chemicals that break down dead material into nutrients and minerals. The mycelia are then able to absorb these things as food.

The mushroom you can see on the forest floor is actually the fruit of the mycelia. But unlike a fruit tree, the mushroom's "branches" (mycelia) grow underground.

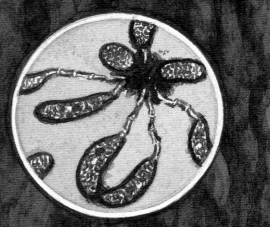

WARNING:
Be a Cautious Mycophagist

A *mycophagist* is someone who eats wild mushrooms. Because so many mushrooms are extremely poisonous, *never* eat a wild one unless you are with experts from a mycological (mushroom) society. As mushroom hunters are fond of saying: There are bold mycophagists, and old mycophagists, but no old, bold mycophagists.

Mushroom Fingerprints

Mushrooms multiply by producing thousands and sometimes millions of tiny *spores*. Spores aren't true seeds but minute cells formed on the *gills* (plates of tissue located under the mushroom's cap). When spores are released, they fall to the forest floor and germinate. Mycelia soon grow from these spores and begin to weave through the forest *leaf litter* (a mix of decomposing leaves, twigs, and animals on top of the soil).

The color and pattern of spores are not only beautiful but they can also help you identify mushrooms. Spore patterns are like fingerprints.

What you need:
mushrooms
knife
several sheets of white paper
several small bowls

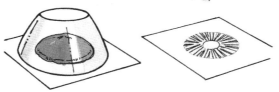

1. Collect several different types of mushrooms with gills.
2. Cut off the mushroom stalk just below the cap.

3. Place several pieces of white paper on a table.
4. Put the mushroom caps, gills down, on the pieces of paper.
5. Cover the mushrooms with the bowls, and leave them overnight.
6. In the morning, remove the bowls and carefully lift the mushroom caps. Spores can blow away, so do this in a spot with no wind.

If you want to preserve your spore prints you can coat them with hair spray or a clear fixative sold in art stores. Warning: Hold the spray can away from your face. Do not inhale the fumes.

Nutrient Recycling

What all those scavengers were doing as they ate the raccoon, besides getting a meal, was helping to return energy to the soil and the forest in the form of minerals, carbohydrates, and nitrogen. As they ate, they helped the raccoon decompose by opening it up to other decomposition creatures and by tearing it into smaller and smaller pieces. They also left behind nitrogen-packed feces.

In some forests, leaf litter can be very thick. Without leaf litter and its host of decomposers, the forest couldn't survive. The dynamic duo of bacteria and fungi join forces to decompose the litter (and raccoon scraps), and, in the process, they begin to break down nitrogen and other nutrients into a form plants can absorb. *Humus* (the layer of dark, fertile soil under the leaf litter) is the product of nature's composting system. Humus is packed with nutrients and microorganisms. It is also the favorite habitat for compost creatures that eat plant materials and microorganisms, leaving behind nutrient-rich droppings.

Greenpatch Kid

Mushroom Hunter

One spring afternoon in Lawrence, Kansas, Sally Kay and her mom were driving home from school. As they passed a wooded area, Sally looked out the window and began yelling, *"Hericium caput-ursi, hericium caput-ursi!"* Her mother stopped the car, and they walked back toward the trees together. Growing in the crotch of a tree was a basketball-sized mushroom. Not only had Sally spotted the mushroom from a moving car, but she properly identified it with its Latin name, *Hericium caput-ursi.* Sally was only four years old!

Her parents were impressed with Sally's discovery, but not surprised. As Sally will tell you, she has been fascinated with mushrooms ever since she can remember: "When I was little, we would go out in the woods and hunt mushrooms. We hunted mostly in Kansas, but we also went to places like Michigan, the New England area, and Illinois."

Today, 16-year-old Sally likes to ride her horse Mincie and play her bass guitar, but mushrooms are still special to her. "I've collected hundreds of different mushroom species over the years," says Sally. "I don't really know the total. My favorite mushrooms are chanterelles because they're a wonderful edible mushroom. They're bright yellowish orange, and some are red. They're kind of shaped like cones tipped upside down. Mushroom hunting is interesting," says Sally. "In fact, mushrooms are like a whole different kingdom. They aren't vegetables, minerals, or animals. They're very unique, and that's interesting. And slime

molds are another kingdom, and they are *very* interesting. The weird thing about slime molds is that they move. Really. They crawl from one place to another, kind of like an amoeba. They only move little by little, but it's still strange."

Mushroom hunting is interesting for Sally, but Sally's and her parents' knowledge of mushrooms is also very important. "I've found plenty of poisonous mushrooms," explains Sally, "like amanitas and lepiotas. Another poisonous mushroom that grows on lawns here is called *Chlorophyllum molybdites.* It's a large white mushroom that's greenish on the underside. It's dangerous because children can eat them by mistake. Sometimes when people get poisoned and go to the hospital, the hospital will call us to ask what species they ate. It's really important to know your poisonous mushrooms." Recently Sally answered such a call when her parents weren't home. As she suspected, the culprit was *Chlorophyllum molybdites.*

Some Exquisite Compost

What happened to the leftovers on your plate from last night? You know, the stuff your dog and your little brother wouldn't eat? What happened to the peels from that orange and banana you munched this morning? What happened to the eggshells from your scrambled eggs? Did they get thrown into the garbage can, or are they outside, right now, being devoured by compost creatures?

Composting is one of the most important things you can do to help the environment. It is also easy and fun. By collecting scraps from your kitchen and plant trimmings from your yard, you will reduce your garbage production while cooking up a rich fertilizer for your garden. By adding compost to your soil, you will increase the number of microorganisms and compost creatures living there, make it easier for your soil to breathe, help your soil retain water and nutrients, and grow monster tomatoes and gorgeous flowers.

Composting is taking place all around you, naturally. When a leaf falls to the soil, it's attacked by bacteria and fungi, and compost creatures arrive for a meal. When you build a compost pile, you are mimicking nature on a grand scale. Whether or not you want a simple pile, a wire basket, or a pull-apart wooden bin, here is an easy guide to making your own compost. Remember, start out small, then think big.

What you need:
compost ingredients (kitchen scraps, yard
   trimmings, manure)
5-gallon bucket with tight-fitting lid
shovel and pitchfork
4-by-4-foot area of ground, some extra soil

How to Find Compost Ingredients

Compost ingredients are all around your kitchen and yard. Keep a bucket with a tight-fitting lid in your kitchen or outside the kitchen door. Dump all fruit and vegetable scraps in that bucket, but *no* meat or dairy products. Add the contents of the bucket to your pile every other day, so the bucket won't get smelly. Collect yard trimmings and leaves. The smaller the ingredients the better, so cut twigs and branches into 1-inch pieces.

Manure from horses, cows, and chickens is a great plus for your pile (but *not* the stuff from you or your dog or cat or wild animals). Your local stable, ranch, riding club, dairy, poultry farm, or zoo may be a good source of animal manure. Bring a strong bag or container, load up, and bring it home. If you can't find animal manure, don't worry. You can still make excellent compost.

Piles

Find a flat 4-by-4-foot area in your yard with good sun exposure. Loosen up this square of soil with the shovel, and water lightly. First, put down a 6-inch layer of straw or leaves (to let the bottom of the pile

"breathe"). Sprinkle a thin layer of soil on top of that. Follow that with 6 inches of animal manure, if available, or more organic material, such as the stuff from the kitchen scrap bucket or your yard. Then repeat the process until your pile is about 3 feet tall. If you are using grass clippings, put them on about 1 inch at a time, because they tend to form a solid mat inside your pile.

When you're done, your pile will look like a huge loaf of bread with braces. Sprinkle it with water. You want your compost to be moist, like a wrung-out sponge, but *not* soaking wet. If it rains a lot where you live, cover the pile with plastic or plywood during storms. Rain is OK, but not too much of it. If it's dry where you live, you might want to sprinkle your pile every other day.

Take a piece of chicken wire and cover your pile. Hold it down on the corners with rocks or bricks. The wire will keep raccoons and other animals from digging up your pile, while permitting your pile to breathe.

Bins

If your yard is small, or you have a lot of nighttime bandits, then you might want to build your pile in a bin. You can do this by making a round bin out of chicken wire, using scrap lumber to make a bin, or buying a bin from a store. Some cities require bins to be rodent-resistant, so check with your local recycling office or health department first.

Wire Bin. Find a piece of wire (chicken wire or 2-by-4-inch welded wire) 4 feet wide and 9 feet long. Stand the piece of wire on edge, loop around the ends, and attach them with pieces of wire or rope. Once assembled, your bin should be 4 feet tall and about 3 feet across. Place your bin on a prepared piece of soil, and add compost ingredients following the "Piles" instructions above. To turn your wire bin pile, lift up the entire bin, move it several feet over, and then scoop the ingredients back in with a pitchfork.

Wooden Bin. Any type of untreated scrap wood can be used to make a compost bin. Leftover pallets from grocery stores and warehouses are perfect for compost bins, and they're often free. The bin should have four sides, be open on the top and bottom, and measure about 4 by 4 feet. The sides should allow for plenty of air circulation. If you want, make it so one side comes off or swings out. That will make turning your compost easier.

1" x 6" boards nailed to posts

4"x4" post
two 1" x 1" boards
Note: construction allows for removable sides.

Store-bought Bin. There are many companies that make compost bins. They come in all shapes, sizes, and materials. Ask at your local gardening center, or pick up a gardening magazine and look for an ad.

Maintenance

When your pile is completed, your compost will start heating up in a day or two, although composting takes place at *all* temperatures. Heat (besides that supplied by the sun) is a by-product of bacteria eating your compost. If your compost never heats up, then add some more organic material to the top of the pile (a sprinkle of fresh grass clippings works well), mix it in, and water. Compost matures faster in warm weather.

Some people make a pile and keep adding to it without ever turning it over. Eventually they harvest mature compost from the bottom of the pile. If you are in no hurry, this system works just fine.

If you want to speed up the decomposition process, then turn your pile once a week, or every time you add kitchen scraps. Take your pitchfork and bring material from the bottom of the pile to the top. Add new ingredients and mix them in. After several months, stop adding new ingredients. Turn your pile for another couple of weeks, then leave it alone for another week. When your compost looks like soil and smells sweet, it's ready.

Do's and Don'ts

Do compost:

vegetable and fruit scraps
eggshells
coffee grounds
tea bags
grass clippings
yard trimmings
leaves
weeds (*before* they flower)
animal manure

Don't compost:

meat scraps
dog, cat, and wild animal feces
cat litter
weeds with seeds
diseased plants
unchopped branches

Greenpatch Kid

Compost King

Patrick O'Donnell takes his composting seriously. If Patrick had his way, his entire neighborhood on New York's Staten Island—and every neighborhood in America—would think composting was a natural thing to do, like waking up, eating, and playing.

"I like composting for a lot of reasons," says Patrick. "Compost is really good for the soil. It also takes a lot of waste off the landfills. I heard something like 14,000 tons of grass clippings go into the landfill here. All that stuff can be composted. Composting also saves money. A bag of good soil costs money. But this way you make your own soil, and it's even better than the stuff you buy. I think *everyone* should compost."

Patrick built a compost pile in his backyard against a fence. "I put most of our yard waste, stuff like leaves, twigs, grass clippings, and some soil, in the compost," explains Patrick. "Then I turn it over about once a week. When it breaks down, the compost goes in my garden. My outside compost has bugs and things in it, but not as many worms as my worm bin."

In a warm, dark corner of Patrick's basement, his worm bin is home to hundreds of red wigglers. "I started out with maybe twenty-five worms," says Patrick. "But they've really multiplied. I put kitchen scraps into the worm bin, like small pieces of apple peelings, banana peelings, and potato skins. So far, I've harvested the worm castings from my bin once. You have to sit

yourself down to do this. You pick out all of the worms, take out the castings, and use the castings where you want to. Then you start all over again with bedding for the worms and kitchen scraps."

Winters can be very cold on Staten Island, but Patrick says the weather doesn't stop his composting activities. "During the wintertime, the outside compost is always biodegrading, so it heats up. It's, like, burning itself, so that keeps the compost warm. And the worm bin is in the basement, so those worms stay plenty warm.

"I think I'll always compost, wherever I go," says Patrick, laughing. "But not if I go on vacation. You can't really take your compost heap on vacation."

As the Worm Turns

If you don't have a yard for outdoor composting, then get a plastic worm bin, and make a worm composter in your apartment, house, or school. Tell your parents not to worry, it won't smell. This is called *vermicomposting* (*vermi* is Latin for worm).

What you need:

plastic worm bin with lid, 1 foot deep by 2 feet wide by 3 feet long
large nail
plastic tray, slightly larger than 2 by 3 feet
topsoil or compost
chopped food scraps
worms

Bins. Many companies sell worm bins. Ask your local garden center or hardware store. You can also make one out of any plastic container with the above dimensions. If you make your own, punch small holes in the bottom of the bin with the nail so excess water can drain out. The lid should also have holes in it to allow plenty of oxygen to reach the worms. Each bin should sit on a plastic tray to catch water.

Bedding. Worm bedding can be made from a variety of chopped-up organic materials. Try mixing a bit of topsoil or compost with shredded newspapers (uncolored) and dried leaves. The bedding should always be moist but not soaked.

Worms. Earthworms from your garden or compost pile work fine in worm bins, but the best worms to use are the small red wigglers. You can buy red wigglers from garden centers and mail-order worm farms.

Maintenance

Once you get your worms, drop them in your bin, close the lid, and let them get to work. Don't let your bin get too cold or too hot. The perfect temperature is somewhere between 55 and 75 degrees Fahrenheit. Feed your worms about twice a week with finely chopped food scraps (no meat). Take off the lid, dig a shallow hole, put in your scraps, then cover with some bedding.

Several times a year, you can harvest the contents of the bin for use in your garden by taking your bin outside and dumping it onto a large plastic sheet. Separate the vermicompost into small piles and carefully remove as many worms as you can. Collect the worms in a can. Rinse out your bin and fill it with fresh bedding. Add the worms and start all over again.

What's Eating You?

There are all sorts of fungi, bacteria, insects, and animals that eat dead things. But did you know some creatures survive by eating small bits of living things without killing them? They are called *parasites*.

That mallard duck you saw in the pond yesterday is probably crawling with feather lice. The duck's stomach and intestines are probably packed with parasitic worms. One researcher found some 1,600 tapeworms of six different types in a single duck! Remember those fence lizards you were watching on the rocks last week? Many of them had small ticks lodged behind their ear openings.

So parasites only live on or in plants and animals, right? Right. But they can also live on and in humans (remember, you're an animal, too). Have you ever curled up with a dog or a cat? If you have, then two of the world's most common parasites probably crawled across your skin: fleas and ticks. And what about that itchy scalp of yours? Did you ever hear of head lice? Bloodsuckers such as fleas, ticks, lice, and mites use the blood they take

from you or other animals for nourishment and to help produce eggs and young.

Perhaps you've seen a picture of a tapeworm. The beef tapeworm can grow 75 feet long, and it just *loves* human intestines. Even as you are reading this, tiny mites could be burrowing into your skin. To parasites, you're just another warm-blooded mammal. Relax. Didn't you know you were feeding your own personal zoo?

Skin Walkers

Most of us live in such clean environments that we have a hard time believing humans can have parasites living on their skin. But whether you live in a high-rise apartment, in the suburbs, or on a ranch, you could be feeding parasites. Parasites that live on your skin are called *ectoparasites* (*ecto* is Greek for "outside").

The vast majority of insects and *arachnids* (spiders and their relatives) are *not* harmful to humans. In fact, most are beneficial to humans. But a few parasitic ones are real pests, and a few of them can be deadly.

In tropical countries, anopheles mosquitoes transmit malaria *protozoa* (microscopic organisms) into humans when they suck blood. It is

You Nitpicker

Do you feel lousy? Maybe it's because you have lice! There are two species of lice that might live on different parts of your body. They are about ⅛ inch long, hang on to your body with strong claws, and suck blood.

Head lice, *Pediculus humanus capitis*, suck blood from your scalp and leave itchy red spots. Female lice lay a daily batch of tiny pale eggs, called *nits*, at the base of hair *follicles* (the places on your skin where individual hairs grow). The eggs hatch in about a week, and the adults can live for several weeks. Head lice are common in children everywhere and are transferred from head to head during play.

Body lice, *Pediculus humanus corporis*, live and lay eggs on clothing. They only crawl on to your skin to feed. Body lice live on people who rarely change their clothes or bathe. Think about that next bath time.

The Mighty Mite

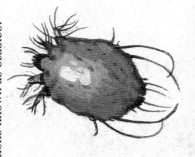

The bothersome mite is a relative of the spider. There are many species of mites, but the most common on humans and pets is the itch or mange mite, *Sarcoptes scabiei*. Females are only ⅟₆₀ inch long, and males are about half that size! Both have mouthparts for penetrating skin and sucking blood.

Female mites burrow into skin to mate with males and to deposit their eggs. Their burrowing, egg laying, and the hatching of their larvae irritate the skin, causing rashes and infections known as scabies.

Are You Ticked Off?

Ticks are only ⅛ inch to ¼ inch long, but they can make you mad. Ticks, which are arachnids, can sit on bushes or the tips of grass blades for months, waiting for a ride. When something rubs against them (like your shoe or leg), they latch on and immediately crawl around looking for skin.

When a tick finds a patch of skin, it burrows its head into the skin and starts sucking blood. Ticks have backward-pointing spines on the sides of their heads that make them difficult to remove. By the time they have had their fill of blood, their saclike abdomen can expand to almost ½ inch. When full, ticks fall off, lay eggs, then die.

estimated that between 400 and 500 million people worldwide suffer from malaria (90 percent of them in Africa). Malaria kills between 1.5 and 3 million people a year.

The infamous Black Death of Europe (also known as the bubonic plague) killed millions of people in Europe during the 14th century. The bubonic plague is caused by the *Yersinia pestis* bacteria transmitted by fleas that live on rats and other rodents but also feed on human blood. This bacteria is still alive in some parts of the world.

Here are a few of the most common pesky parasites you might encounter:

Your Dog Has Fleas

There are about 1,000 species of fleas in the world. Two of the most common species are *Ctenocephalides canis* and *C. felis*. *C. canis* lives on dogs and *C. felis* lives on cats. But when your pooch or kitty isn't around, these little blood-suckers will move on to the closest warm body—you. There is also the less common human flea, *Pulex irritans*, that can be found on people and animals.

Fleas don't have wings, but some species have been known to jump 13 inches. If one lands on you, it will use its siphonlike sucking tube to penetrate your skin and drink your blood.

Internal Invaders

In many parts of the world, humans live full lives while feeding an internal population of parasitic worms and other foreign microscopic organisms. Parasites that live in your body are called *endoparasites* (*endo* is Greek for "within"). There are countless types of endoparasites and all have complicated life cycles.

Many enter human bodies through infected drinking water or undercooked meat. All endoparasites have protective coatings on their bodies so they can live in your intestines or other organs without being digested by your body's acids and enzymes.

Here are two common endoparasites you might encounter as you pass through life as a warm-blooded mammal.

Tapeworms

Tapeworms are ribbon-shaped worms that live in animal and human intestines. Adult tapeworms have suckers or hooks on their heads that they use for attaching to the inside wall of the intestines. Tapeworms don't have mouths for eating. Instead, they absorb the predigested food in the intestines through the surface of their entire body.

There are many different types of tapeworms that can live in humans. Animals that humans eat—cattle, sheep, pigs, and fish—ingest tapeworm eggs from the soil, grass, or water. Once inside the animal's intestines, minute tapeworm larvae hatch and burrow into muscle tissue. Humans eat the animal meat *and* the larvae. If the meat isn't cooked enough, the larvae survive and grow into

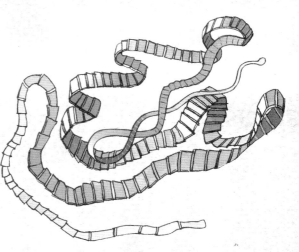

adult tapeworms inside your intestines, where they produce millions of eggs that leave your body in your feces. In unsanitary conditions, the eggs are consumed by animals, and the cycle continues.

Although the beef tapeworm can grow to a length of 75 feet, most range from 1 inch to 20 feet long. This sounds scary, but people with tapeworms rarely get very sick. Instead they come down with stomachaches or diarrhea. Feel a bit queasy? Don't fret. Diagnosis and treatment by a doctor are easy.

tapeworm eggs

Giardia

Giardia is a microscopic protozoan, *Giardia lamblia*, that exists everywhere in the world and is one of the most common parasites known to humans. Giardia is also known as a *flagellate* (a small creature that moves about with the help of small flagella).

This parasite is spread by contaminated water or food, or by hand-to-mouth contact. Most people with giardia don't have symptoms, but others have diarrhea, cramps, nausea, and *flatus* (a fancy word for gas). Giardia comes to rest in your intestines, where it receives nourishment and reproduces. You then pass the protozoan in your feces. In unsanitary conditions, the cycle then starts all over again.

What to Do with Unwanted Visitors

If you think you have any external or internal visitors, tell a grown-up, and they can call a doctor. *Don't panic.* All parasites are easily removed, but you have to know how to do it properly. And in most developed countries with good sanitation, these unwanted visitors are rare.

giardia

Diseases and Defenders

Parasites come and go *on* and *in* the human body. But sometimes diseases affect the body and don't leave. When this happens, the body goes on full alert and fights to survive.

Diseases are caused by a variety of germs (known formally as *pathogens*), such as harmful bacteria, viruses, or toxins. Your body has many barriers to keep out germs: a tough outer layer of skin; protective cells lining your air passages, stomach, and intestines; and enzymes in your tears that kill harmful types of bacteria.

But if a germ is persistent and it breaks through your defenses, your body's *immune system* reacts like a fire station when an alarm sounds. At the fire station, firefighters sprint to get ready, the fire engines are revved up, and the equipment is checked. Within minutes the engines and fighters are zooming toward the fire to put it out. When your body "hears" a disease alarm, your immune system sends *white blood cells* racing to the scene to attack the germ.

Powerful Internal Scavengers

White blood cells (WBCs) are like internal scavengers you carry around with you at all times. They move throughout your body detecting harmful foreign invaders. There are about 7,500 WBCs for every cubic millimeter of your blood, and they are only 15 thousandths of a millimeter in diameter, but they are very strong fighters. Red blood cells (RBCs), which carry oxygen from your lungs to your body's tissues and exchange it for carbon dioxide, are about 7.5 thousandths of a millimeter in diameter. There are some 5 million RBCs in a cubic millimeter of blood!

There are different types of WBCs, but all are attracted to chemical substances called *antigens* that germs produce. When antigens are detected on the outer cell wall of a germ, they trigger your body's immune system.

When you have a bad cut and it gets infected, WBCs move to the area to clean it up. After a while, the cut becomes swollen with a mixture of dead tissue, bacteria cells, and living and dead WBCs that form a gooey liquid called *pus*. Pus may look gross, but it shows that your body is hard at work fighting the infection.

tears

stomach lining

intestinal villi

skin

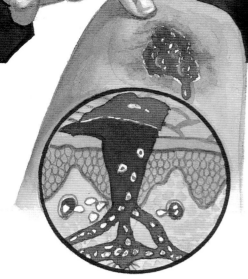

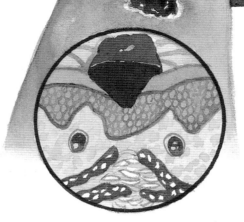

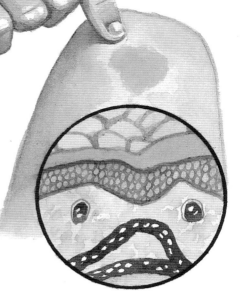

Cut is filled with blood, dead cells, and dirt. Scab begins to form.

Repair and regrowth take place beneath scab. WBCs clean up. Pus may form.

New cells form, repairing cut.

Antibodies, Anybody?

When WBCs confront a real tough germ, they may produce specific *antibodies* to attack its antigens. Antibodies are special proteins formed by WBCs when cells in your body are exposed to germs that contain antigens. The antibodies are custom-made by your body to fit with the antigen like a key fits a lock. The next time the germ (and its antigens) comes along to cause a disease, the antibody finds it and fits in the lock to activate your immune response. When an antibody tracks down a germ, it either wraps around it, disabling it, or completely kills the germ by destroying its cell wall.

Why Germs?

It might be hard to believe, but germs—and parasites—are part of Earth's natural system. They are living organisms that have adapted survival techniques that include using humans for a food source or a safe place to reproduce.

Archaeologists studying ancient burial sites have discovered that disease-causing germs and humans have *always* been together. But it wasn't until humans settled down into small communities, and eventually cities, that germs became a serious problem. Many early cities were crowded and dirty places. They were a perfect environment for germs to spread easily from person to person. As humans began exploring the world, they carried their germs with them. Today, germs are still traveling around the world with the help of people.

Kiss a Cow, Take a Vaccine

Your body can produce special antibodies for each disease-causing germ it encounters. Once they are formed and the disease is cured, antibodies stay with you to prevent future infections. To help people from getting sick the first time around, *vaccines* were developed beginning in the 19th century.

Scientists learned that animals injected with small amounts of livestock germs became ill for a little while, then improved. If they were injected later with the same germs, the animals showed no signs of the disease. When a vaccine is injected into the body, the body reacts by forming antibodies that are specifically designed to combat that small dose of germs. Many of these first experiments used cows, therefore the term *vaccine* (*vacca* is Latin for "cow").

You can also get a shot of *antiserum*, which contains a load of ready-formed antibodies. Antiserum is produced by injecting a germ into some other animal, waiting until the animal has produced antibodies against that germ, and then removing those antibodies from the animal and using them in humans.

Antibiotics (drugs used for infections caused by bacteria), like penicillin, were originally made from molds and fungi, many of which were discovered growing in soil. Today, their chemistry is well known, and these antibiotics are produced by using synthetic ingredients.

The Death of Mr. Soto

Mr. Soto had a million friends, and almost all of them were made across the counter of his small grocery store and delicatessen on the edge of downtown. Even on the stormiest or hottest day, even when the traffic was jammed for miles outside his store, the jovial Mr. Soto would greet *every* customer with, "It's a beautiful day, no?" Mr. Soto loved life.

No one kept track, but it seemed like Mr. Soto spoke a dozen languages. "Just call me the Rainbow Kid," he would tell you, one arm resting on the counter, the other holding a cigarette, "since my ancestors were so many different colors." His father's grandfather sailed from China, settled in the South American port city of Guayaquil, and married an Indian woman from a small village high above the clouds in the Andes Mountains. Mr. Soto didn't know how his grandfather arrived in the United States, or whom he married. Mr. Soto's grandfather on his mother's side was Lebanese, and he married a woman from Brazil, who "came from the Amazon somewhere." Mr. Soto loved mysteries.

At the end of a hot and humid day, Mr. Soto got up from a large meal and walked into the store (his family had a small kitchen off the back of the store). Mr. Soto loved to eat, and his large belly proved it. He lit a cigarette, picked up his old broom, and started sweeping.

Without warning, Mr. Soto felt a sudden pain—just as if someone had hit him in the chest real hard. He dropped the broom and cigarette and clutched his breastbone. As the viselike force increased, he broke out into a cold sweat. The pressure moved down his left arm and into his throat. Mr. Soto could barely breathe. He tried walking to the store counter, but he couldn't move his feet. The pressure became too painful and Mr. Soto collapsed to the unswept floor.

Just then a neighborhood kid, Ronald Jones (everyone called him Ronjo), bounced into the store to buy a quart of milk. He saw Mr. Soto sprawled on the floor, eyes open. "Mr. Soto!" Ronjo called out as he ran over to him. Ronjo got down on the floor and shook Mr. Soto's shoulder. Mr. Soto didn't answer.

Ronjo sprinted out of the store and onto the sidewalk, yelling for help. A neighborhood policeman heard Ronjo and rushed to the scene. The policeman saw Mr. Soto and immediately called for an ambulance. When the paramedics arrived, fifteen minutes after he had collapsed, it was too late. Mr. Soto lay on the floor, expressionless. His eyes were glazed over, and his wide-open black pupils stared upward at the multicolored piñatas hanging from the ceiling. Mr. Soto was dead.

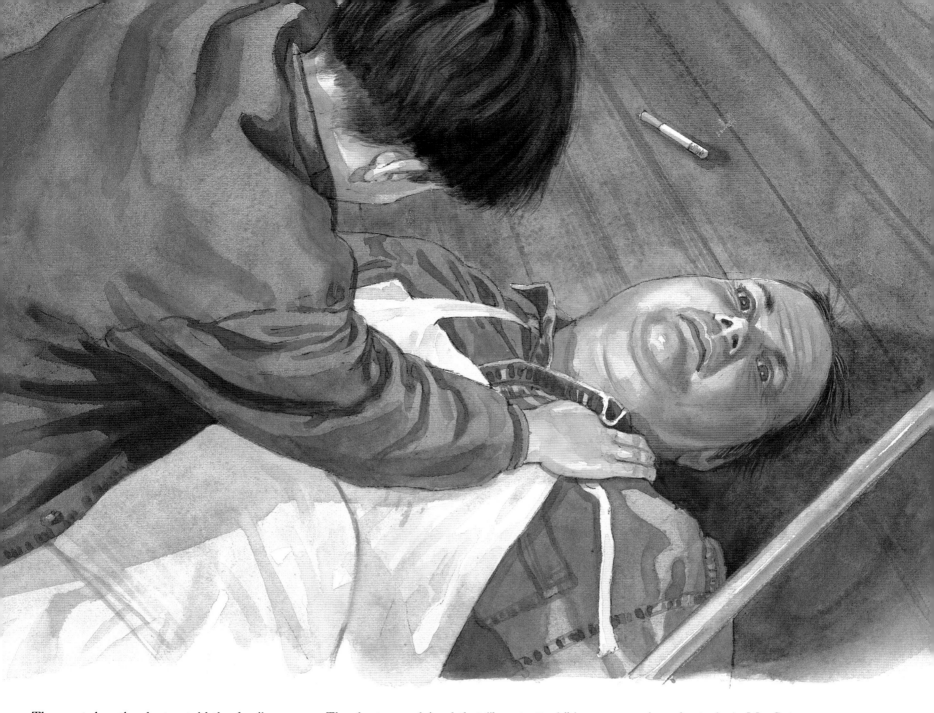

The next day, the doctor told the family that Mr. Soto died from a heart attack, or a *myocardial infarction*. This news brought a sad smile to all of Mr. Soto's neighborhood friends. "Mr. Soto's heart was *so* big," said one, "that it was too big for his body." Little did his friends know this diagnosis was partially correct: Mr. Soto's damaged heart had grown slightly larger than most during the past few years as it strained to pump blood to his brain and throughout his body.

The doctor explained that "heart attack" is one term that describes many different types of heart failures. Mr. Soto's heart died because it was not getting enough *hemoglobin*, a protein that carries oxygen in the blood. His heart was not getting enough hemoglobin because it was not getting enough blood, and it was not getting enough blood because his heart's vessels—the *coronary arteries*—were hardened, narrowed, and damaged by a disease called *arteriosclerosis* (the hardening and

narrowing of arteries). Mr. Soto was a very nice person, but he didn't take good care of his body. Years of no exercise, too much weight, cigarette smoking, and *high blood pressure* (abnormally high pressure in the arteries) caused the arteriosclerosis.

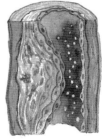

healthy
artery

unhealthy
artery

When his oxygen-starved heart went into convulsions that late afternoon, it stopped pumping blood to his brain. Mr. Soto fell to the floor—he "passed out"—because his brain (the body's command center) couldn't operate his body properly without oxygen. Within 10 minutes his brain was dead. After his brain died, all his major organs (lungs, liver, and kidneys) also died.

Unfortunately, Mr. Soto's story is far too common. Almost 5 million Americans are diagnosed every year with a variety of heart diseases. Over 500,000 Americans die from heart diseases annually.

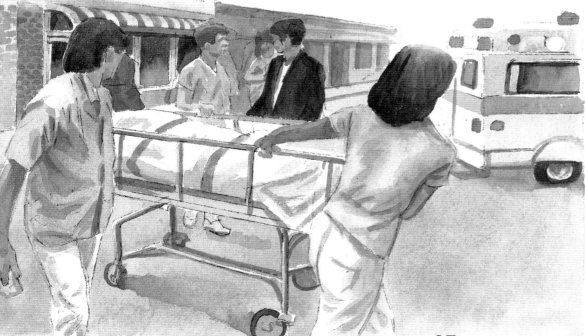

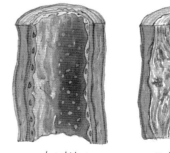

When Is Dead, Dead?

Mr. Soto died because his heart couldn't pump blood to his body's powerful control center—his brain. When his brain stopped functioning and died, the rest of his body died soon after. Mr. Soto died of a heart attack, just like many other people. But no two people ever die precisely the same death. Every person is slightly different when they come into this world; they are just as different in the way they leave.

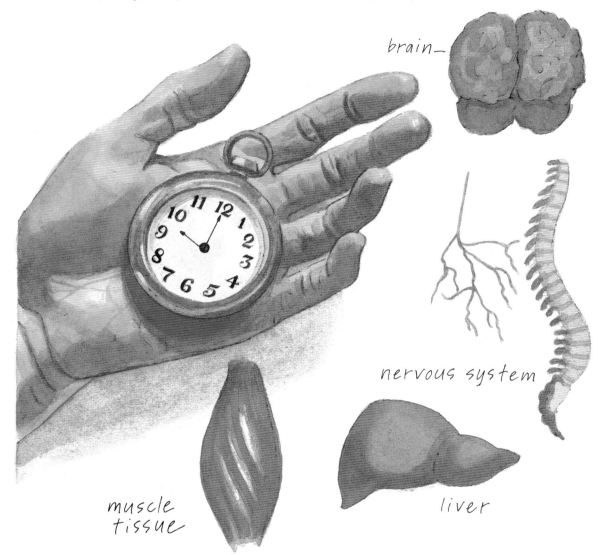

brain

nervous system

muscle tissue

liver

Systems Support

Do heart transplant patients die for a while when a doctor removes the damaged heart and puts in a healthy one? No. They don't die because they are attached to a heart-lung machine. This machine keeps their blood circulating and their lungs breathing.

People who have suffered severe injuries and damage to their central nervous system are often rushed to a hospital and attached to a machine to keep them alive. Their lower brain may still be alive, but their body has lost the ability to function on its own. There is no way to bring a dying or dead brain back to life. It is difficult for families and doctors to decide what to do with a person like this.

Should patients be kept alive by a machine, or should the rest of their body be allowed to die if their condition worsens? More and more, the answers to these questions are being decided by laws, and whether or not the patient signed a *living will* (a document that explains that they do, or do not, wish to be kept alive by machines in case of an accident).

Systems Shutdown

When blood stops circulating throughout a person's body, the body begins to die because it is no longer receiving oxygen. Although heart failure is the main reason blood circulation ends, there are many others.

Regardless of the reason, the *central nervous system* (brain, spinal cord, and nerves) is the first body system to die when blood stops circulating. The brain is like a high-powered engine that constantly needs fuel, and it's *very* sensitive about its oxygen supply. It receives its fuel from a steady supply of oxygen-rich blood. Oxygen is transported to individual brain and body cells by blood. Cell waste products, such as carbon dioxide, are carried away by the blood. When blood stops flowing, the brain can suffocate and die within 5 to 15 minutes.

If blood circulation is severely reduced but not stopped (like after *some* heart attacks or serious injuries), within minutes the outer portion of the brain—the *cerebral cortex*—begins to die. But the lower portions of the brain that control automatic body functions, such as breathing and heartbeat—the *cerebellum* and *brain stem*—can live on with a reduced blood flow. When blood stops circulating completely, the lower brain also dies, and so do all the organs it controls.

Muscle tissues are the last to die after circulation stops. Hours after final death, some muscles will twitch and tighten if touched with electricity. And a few organs, such as the liver, can work without oxygen—a condition called *anaerobic* (Greek for "without air life")—for hours before stopping.

So, even though a person is dead, certain cells within the dead body take a while longer to die. Some muscle, skin, and bone cells may live for days. But this does not mean that the hair and nails of dead people keep growing for days and days. That widely held belief is not true.

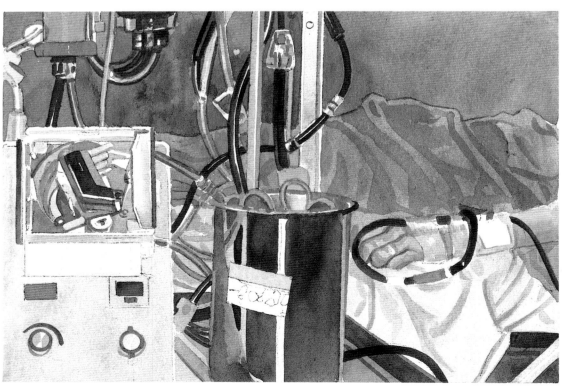

Legal Death

To be declared dead by a doctor in the United States, a strict set of guidelines must be met, following a law called the Uniform Determination of Death Act.

The body must be completely unreceptive and unresponsive. The body does not react to external stimulation (noise and pinch).

The body must not move or breathe for at least one hour.

The body must have no reflexes, such as the reaction of eye pupils to a bright light.

If an *electroencephalogram* (EEG) is performed (an optional procedure) to measure the presence of brain waves, the EEG must be "flat." A flat EEG means the brain is dead.

When Dead Isn't

Can you imagine getting your leg stuck in some rocks and snapping it off at the knee? If that happened, you'd be permanently damaged, and maybe even die. But not if you were a salamander or a lizard. Salamanders and lizards routinely grow spare parts.

If a salamander loses a leg to a hungry raccoon, a mass of nerve fibers soon begins to grow out of its spinal cord toward the healing wound. At first a bump appears. And then, over a period of weeks, the bump stretches into a leg as cells in the area divide into new joints, muscle, and bone.

If a cat swats a lizard, the lizard can make its tail fall off and wiggle to distract the cat. The ability to drop a body part like this is called *autotomy* (Greek for "self cut"). After the tail drops, special muscles squeeze the body at the wound to prevent bleeding. The lizard then grows a new tail. The new tail is smaller than the original, and instead of bone inside it is supported by *cartilage* (the same stuff that makes your nose firm).

Most animals have the ability to regenerate body parts when they are *embryos* (in the early stages of growth before birth). But some animals, such as salamanders and lizards, and also worms and sea stars, can grow new body parts as adults.

If one of your two kidneys has to be removed, then the remaining organ will enlarge and increase its capacity to filter more blood. If a small section of your heart is damaged, other portions of your heart may enlarge to compensate for the damage. This process is called *hypertrophy*. Unlike the lizard and salamander, however, you can't generate *new* cells to grow new body parts. Hypertrophy is just the enlargement of a body part.

Plants have the ability to grow roots from the open end of a cutting. One reason they can do this is because plant cells are totipotent; that is, each cell has all the information in it to become a complete plant. Cells in other organisms are very specific, like nose cells or tail cells. But each plant cell, even if it's located on the cut end of a branch, has enough root information to grow new roots.

Insect Detectives

The human body goes through stages of decomposition after death, just like any other animal. If a person dies outside, exposed and isolated, they become just like the old raccoon that died on the forest floor. And just like the old raccoon, a human body attracts a wide range of insects.

Forensic entomologists (scientists who study insects to determine when and how someone died) can figure out the time of death, and sometimes who killed them (if they were murdered).

Fly species are *always* the first insects to find a dead body, usually within a few hours. And since it is known that maggots take approximately three weeks to mature, and their stages of growth are well known, forensic entomologists can study the maggots, determine their age, and count backward to calculate the time of death.

And because flies are followed on the body by other insects (beetles, spiders, mites, and centipedes) in a precise sequence, these other insects can be used as additional clues.

39

What Does a Mortician

No one likes the idea of being around a dead body, except perhaps a *mortician*. After a person dies, the body is examined by a doctor and then delivered to a mortician. Morticians (also known as undertakers or funeral directors) are the professionals who prepare a body for burial or cremation.

Postmortem

Before being delivered to a mortician, a *corpse* (dead body) is sometimes studied by a doctor. One of the first *postmortem* (Latin for "after death") procedures with a corpse is the *autopsy* (Greek for "seeing with one's own eyes"). Autopsies are performed so doctors can study, or "see," why the person died.

The corpse's entire body and internal organs are examined so that living people may benefit from knowledge gathered by the doctor. Autopsies were once very common in the United States, but today they are performed on less than 15 percent of people who die "normal" deaths. The reasons for this decline vary from state to state, but they include legal and religious concerns, and the belief that modern medical technology has become much better at determining the cause of death without an autopsy. If the cause of death is suspicious or associated with a crime, then autopsies are almost always carried out.

Embalming

The most common way to preserve a body for burial in the United States is by *embalming*. Embalming is the replacement of the body's blood and other fluids with chemical preservatives and disinfectants.

An ancient form of embalming was practiced in China and Egypt over 4,000 years ago. It was also used with European royalty and by some Native American societies. Today, modern embalming is practiced mostly in the United States, Canada, Australia, and England. Embalming is practiced in these countries for two main reasons: public health concerns and ceremonial public viewing for family and friends. Many countries use a variety of ways to prepare their dead, including immediate burial of the body into the ground.

Embalming doesn't permanently preserve corpses. Embalmed bodies still decompose, but they do so in a strange way. After an embalmed corpse is buried, most of the embalming fluid sinks to the back of the body. Researchers have discovered that the front of the body decomposes much faster than the saturated back side. But the corpse *is* preserved long enough to be displayed at a funeral if the family wishes.

The Perfect Tan

Peat bogs (marshes containing dense mats of partially decomposed vegetation) are found across much of northern Europe. Bog water is naturally acidic and full of *tannins* (substances used to "tan," or preserve, animal hides).

For centuries, people have dried out blocks of peat to use as heating fuel. Occasionally, solitary workers died in the bogs. After they collapsed, they fell into the dark brown waters and disappeared. Some of these folks—known today as Bog People—have been discovered in old peat bogs two thousand years after their death! Because they were immediately soaked with tannins, their bodies are almost perfectly preserved and dyed a golden tan.

Rigor Mortis

Not only is a mortician's job rather gruesome, but sometimes it's hard. Within two to six hours after death, bodies stiffen into a condition know as *rigor mortis* (Latin for "stiff death"). That's why a corpse is sometimes referred to as a "stiff." The exact causes of rigor mortis are not known, but it's believed to be produced by the solidifying of proteins within the muscles. Corpses with rigor mortis have to be massaged by the mortician and manipulated back into normal shape before embalming or burial—not an easy job.

Undertake?

How Dry I Am

Everyone has seen a mummy. You know, that horror movie dude wrapped in dusty bandages with the funny walk, who is always chasing people and grunting? Actually, over 4,000 years ago, Egyptians began mummification to preserve their leaders, the pharaohs.

Egyptians created an elaborate and lengthy process to clean and dry a body before placing it in a wooden *sarcophagus* (a large, fancy coffin) and sometimes inside a pyramid. The word *sarcophagus* is Greek and means "flesh-eating stone." It was once believed that limestone sarcophagi helped decompose the corpse, hence the name.

Mummification can happen naturally in dry regions of the world. People who died in warm, dry caves, in deserts, or high in the arid Andes Mountains have been discovered in one piece thousands of years later.

From Fire to Ice

In 1991, a couple of tourists were glacier hiking along the Italian-Austrian border at about 10,500 feet and discovered a human body. They thought the body might have been a murder victim, but scientists soon realized the body was that of a Copper Age hunter or shepherd.

After studying the body, scientists determined it was about 5,000 years old. This unfortunate young man (nicknamed Ötzi, after the Ötztal valley just north of the site) was about 30 years old when he died. Ötzi was so well preserved that the scientists found tattoos on his skin.

Today, some people who wish to live forever have their bodies frozen after they die by a process called *cryonic suspension*. They hope that science will discover a way to defrost them in the future and make them live again. As of now, however, cryonic suspension is only an experiment, because there is no way to make a frozen body come back to life.

Burial

People have been burying their dead since the beginning of time. Early people may have done so to keep animals from eating the bodies, but today people have funerals and bury their dead in elaborate ceremonies.

After a body is prepared for burial (dressed and often embalmed), it is placed in a container called a *coffin* (also known as a *casket*). Coffins are made from a variety of materials, but most are wood or metal. Some bodies and coffins are buried without a ceremony. But some families have an open-casket viewing of the corpse, church services, graveside readings, and prayers before burying the body and coffin.

Today the term "burial at sea" means the scattering of a corpse's ashes over the side of a boat or from an airplane. But it used to be that entire bodies, sewn into canvas bags or placed in a casket, were slid into the open ocean. The bodies had to be weighed down with rocks or cannonballs to make them sink. During the 19th century, this was a common practice on military ships.

About 2 million Americans die every year, and most are buried in the ground. These new graves, if placed side by side, would cover about 1,250 acres, or approximately 2 square miles of ground! That's the equivalent of about 875 football fields. Open space is becoming increasingly rare in the United States. Because of this, the expansion of cemeteries is becoming an important issue in crowded places. Is burying our dead in the ground the best way to go?

Cremains

The human body is 60 percent water. The rest is made up of bone and soft tissue. If a corpse is burned, the water evaporates, and the bone and soft tissue are reduced to *cremains* (ashes and a few small bone fragments). When an adult is cremated, between 4 and 8 pounds of cremains are produced.

Cremation (from a Latin word "to burn") is an ancient way to dispose of a corpse. In early cremation ceremonies around the world, the corpse was placed on top of a pile of wood called a *pyre*. The wood was lit on fire, and the corpse was cremated.

After these early cremations, some bones were left intact. The remains were collected and disposed of with a special ceremony. This method of cremation is still used in parts of Asia and some remote regions of the world.

Modern cremation, which is very popular around the world, takes place in a *crematorium*, a building equipped with special ovens. Corpses are placed inside the crematorium's furnace for about three hours at about 2,000 degrees Fahrenheit. The cremains are then placed in a container and either buried, scattered, or put in a building called a *columbarium*.

The Magnificent Cell

Every minute of the day, millions of cells die inside and on the outside of you. But don't worry. Not only are you the owner of trillions of living cells of about 200 different types, you're not going to *desquamate* (peel away, cell by cell). Those dead parts of you are replaced immediately by new ones. In fact, the death of cells is necessary for you to continue growing and living.

Cells are the building blocks of life, and *all* living things—people, plants, and animals—are made from them. There is still a lot that scientists don't understand about how cells work, but they do know that they come into being, have a life, then die, just like you.

It's hard to believe, but your life began as a single cell that was smaller than the period at the end of this sentence. An *ovum* (an egg cell) from your mother was fertilized by a *sperm* (another cell) from your father. Together, they formed a *zygote* (a single fertilized ovum). The zygote divided into 2 new cells after one day, then 8 cells after three days, then 64 cells after four days. Before long, things started getting crowded in there.

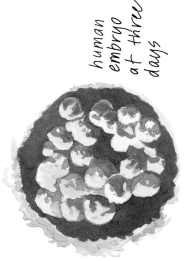

human embryo at three days

Cells reproduce, specialize, and die quickly. As they do, they become distinct parts of you. When you were born, just one of your arms had approximately 43 muscles, 29 bones, and hundreds of nerves—all made from that single zygote. That process of cell division by your body is still going on.

only take a few hours to divide and replace their dying and dead neighbors.

Other cells take longer to divide, while still others, like mature brain cells, *never* reproduce. After your brain has grown to its mature size (but *not* stopped learning, right?) between the ages of five and ten, brain cells just change their parts, like the spark plugs and oil in a car engine. In fact, after you've lived about 50 years, your brain actually gets smaller every year as different cells age, shrink, die, and are not replaced.

Cells divide and reproduce according to set internal time schedules. But these schedules can also be adaptable. If, for example, you lose a lot of blood in an accident or during an operation, your body will immediately detect the loss and go into overtime production of red blood cells. When your red blood cell count is back to normal, your body will resume its regular production schedule.

There is a lot of cell division and dying going on inside and outside of you, and yet, when you're a grown-up, your total cell count stays about the same. It can stay the same because most (but not all) of your cells are constantly replacing themselves.

Cell Wonders

Except for that zygote you divided from, cells are microscopic. On average, the diameter of your cells is somewhere between .5 and 40 microns (a micron is a thousandth of a millimeter). That's small.

An impressive exception to cell size is the yolk of a bird egg—the yellow center of a

organelle, a kind of information center, called a *nucleus*. Inside the nucleus are twisting strands of *deoxyribonucleic acid*, more commonly known as DNA. DNA is attached in bundles called *genes* to one of your 46 *chromosomes* (23 came from your mother, 23 from your father). Scientists don't know for sure, but they believe there might be up to 500,000 genes in a single human cell!

DNA is the cell's code; it holds genetic information, such as your hair color, your height, and the size and shape of your ears. DNA tells the cell what it is going to help build, how, and where. When someone says to you, "Well, no wonder you have red hair, it's in your genes," they aren't talking about your pants.

When a cell divides during mitosis, every part is exactly reproduced according to the genetic information in the nucleus. That means that before division, all of your genes are precisely reproduced in every single new cell, and every organelle is duplicated.

There are many organelles inside a cell, but what is going on outside of a cell, and between cells, is also very important. Throughout your body, cells are suspended in a nutrient-rich soup called *extracellular fluid*. This fluid is made up of one part *blood plasma* (the fluid part of blood that contains proteins, minerals, and salts), and four parts *interstitial fluid* (the liquid around each cell). These fluids are constantly cleaned and replenished by your circulating blood. If you weigh, say, 75 pounds, then about 11 pints of these fluids are floating around the cells of your body.

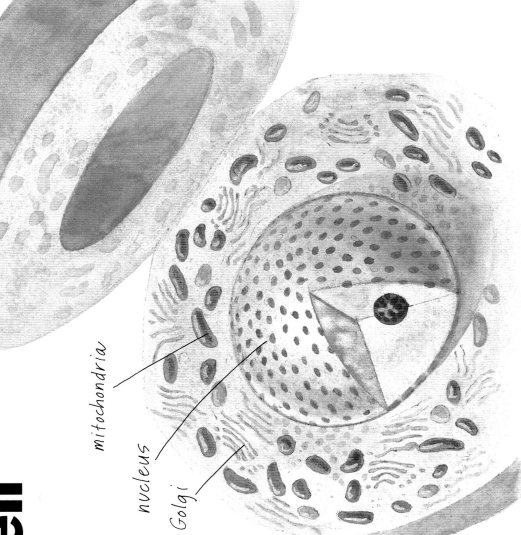

mitochondria
nucleus
Golgi

The Circle of Life

Each cell in your body was formed, will get old, and will die. All plants, animals, and people you know will grow, become old, and eventually die. Death is just as normal and just as important in the circle of life as birth. All living things die, and, in one form or another, return to the earth.

In a sense, all things, living and dead, depend on each other. From organisms that have only one cell, to humans that have trillions of them, any living thing must die and return to the flow of nutrients that cycle endlessly through Earth's ecosystems.

The air the dinosaurs breathed millions of years ago is a part of the air you are breathing right now. The water you drink today once supported the lives of your great-grandparents. What you are, and what you become, is at least partly a result of everything that has come before you. Birth and death are not unrelated events. Life is birth, death, and everything in between. Unless we interfere with it, it continues in a great circle.

chicken egg, for example. This yolk is one big cell. If the egg is fertilized, the yolk helps feed the dividing bird cells and eventually the bird embryo. That means that the yolk of an ostrich egg is about 1,500 times bigger than that zygote you came from!

Most human cells are microscopic, but they are *very* complicated. If you were to look through a powerful electron microscope (they can magnify objects up to 250,000 times larger than their normal size), here is some of what you might see.

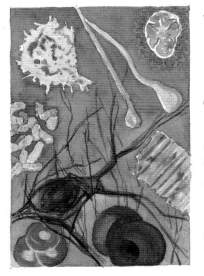

Programmed Cell Death

Believe it or not, you had gills and a small tail when you first formed. That's right. You looked just like a newly formed fish or chicken for a while. But luckily, your tail and gill cells died, thanks to a process called Programmed Cell Death (PCD).

Scientists now believe PCD is critical for the growth and health of your entire body. For example, five weeks after your zygote formed your hands looked like small Ping-Pong paddles. During the next two weeks, strips of cells on each paddle died. As they died, spaces formed between your fingers. After about eight weeks, you had complete tiny fingers. As some cells died, other ones reproduced into new parts, and you began to look human.

When you were developing as a zygote, and now as you grow as a kid, and then later as an adult, cells are and will be constantly dying. When they die, the cells break up into fragments and are absorbed and recycled by neighboring cells. Without this cell death, you wouldn't grow at all.

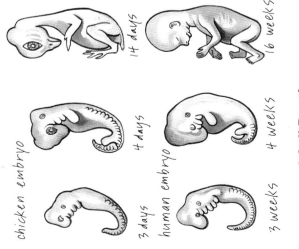

chicken embryo
3 days   4 days   14 days
human embryo
3 weeks   4 weeks   6 weeks

Cell Cycles

To reproduce, cells divide into exact copies of themselves by a process called *mitosis*. Different kinds of cells live for differing amounts of time, but the cells that divide and reproduce the most are those on the interior walls of your intestines, on your skin, and around your hair follicles. These cells may

Cells come in all shapes. Some are round, while others are square. Some look like tadpoles, while others are doughnut-shaped (but without the hole). Some nerve cells are amazingly thin but stretch for 3 to 4 feet inside of you! Yet others look like jiggling drops of jelly that continually change their shape.

Regardless of their shape and size, all cells are packed into a skin called a *plasma membrane*. Inside are *organelles*—cell parts that help the cell feed, get rid of waste, reproduce, form everything from hair follicles to big toes, and eventually die.

At the heart of each cell is a memory bank

This Junk Called Garbage

Garbage has been around almost as long as people have been. Thousands of years ago, humans simply threw their garbage in one spot near their campsite or village. When the junk pile got too big or messy, they moved their camp or built on top of it.

The Romans are believed to be the first people to make laws requiring garbage to be brought to dumps away from their city. Ancient, and not-so-ancient, garbage dumps can tell scientists a lot about how people lived—how they cooked, what they hunted, grew, and ate, and what they made.

Yesterday's garbage is today's archaeological treasure chest. Today's garbage is a big headache. Today, there is too much junk.

Find a Hole and Fill It

Today's dumps are called *landfills* by garbage professionals. Instead of exposed heaps of junk, landfills are engineered so runoff doesn't pollute nearby waterways, and the garbage is covered with a layer of soil every now and again and then compressed by huge tractors.

But no matter how well designed today's dumps are, humans still produce too much junk. On average, you will throw away about 5 pounds of garbage *every* day. That adds up to some 400,000 tons daily across the U.S. Most of that still goes to dumps.

And if you are like most Americans, you will produce about 600 times your own weight in garbage during your lifetime. That's more than twice as much junk produced by the average Japanese or German citizen. Every three months, we throw away enough aluminum to rebuild the United States' entire commercial fleet of jetliners. Each year office workers throw away enough paper to build a 12-foot-tall wall that would stretch across the U.S., and we toss enough plastic soda bottles to circle Earth *four* times if they were placed end to end.

Why do people today, and *especially* Americans, produce so much junk? Our consumer society encourages us to always buy *new* things, not reuse *old* ones. And although recycling is becoming more popular, and easier, there is much more we can do.

Garbageologist

Conduct a household garbage audit and find out what kind of garbage you produce. By doing so, you can discover what you could be reusing and recycling.

What you need:
garbage can full of garbage
plastic sheet, 10 by 10 feet
gloves
shovel
dust mask (optional)

1. Take your full garbage can (best the day *before* the garbage pickup) to a flat spot outside.
2. Spread out your sheet of plastic.
3. Dump the can's contents into the middle of the sheet. It might be a bit stinky, but who said being a garbageologist would smell good?
4. Put on your gloves and separate your garbage into piles: paper, glass, plastic, metal, food scraps, and miscellaneous.

How many items from these piles could be reused around the house, recycled, repaired and sold, given to a charitable organization, or composted? You will discover that you are throwing away things you don't need to.

When you are done with your audit, shovel the garbage back into the can. Wash down the plastic sheet, let it dry, fold it up, and save it for another use in the future.

After your garbage audit, call city hall and find out who picks up your garbage and where it goes. Most dumps or transfer stations (where garbage is dumped, processed, then sent to a landfill) will let you come watch the operation. Many will also give you tips on how to reduce your household garbage.

Rot Time

If today's dumps were filled with just organic stuff—plant material and food scraps—they would break down relatively fast. But they aren't. Today's dumps are going to be with us, in one form or another, for a long time. Different types of junk take different amounts of time to decompose. Take a look.
Paper scraps: 2–4 weeks
Wool mittens: 1 year
Painted wood: 13 years
Tin can: 100 years
Aluminum can: 200–500 years
Plastic six-pack rings: 450 years
Glass bottle: 1,000+ years

When Junk Isn't

Most of today's garbage still ends up down in the dumps. But land for dumps is diminishing, especially around large cities. Even more importantly, when garbage is buried in the ground, we are throwing away natural resources: wood, metals, and composting ingredients.

It takes *less* energy and it's *less* polluting to recycle natural resources from garbage than it is to make new products from raw materials. For example, recycling one glass jar saves enough energy to power a 100-watt light bulb for four hours. Aluminum is made from a natural resource called bauxite. But recycling aluminum requires 95 percent less energy, results in 95 percent less air pollution, and 97 percent less water pollution than producing new aluminum by mining bauxite. If all Americans recycled their newspapers for just one Sunday, we could save the equivalent of 550,000 trees!

The Solution: Reduce, Reuse, Recycle

Your ancestors were excellent recyclers and reusers. Just 100 years ago, people produced little garbage because everything was a valuable resource. There were no fast-food restaurants or convenience stores. Scrap metals, newspapers, glass jars, and many other materials were saved and put to other uses. Old clothes were patched and used by many different children. Rags were used to make beautiful quilts.

Your ancestors were recyclers and reusers because they *had* to be; it was how they did things back then. It can be that way again: recycling and reusing can become second nature to you, like knowing how to tie your shoes or make compost.

You can use the three Rs—reduce, reuse, recycle—every day as you go about your business. Learn your three Rs, and you can begin to make Earth a cleaner and safer place to be.

Reduce. The best way to reduce your consumption of products is to be a smart shopper (your ancestors didn't have to worry about this because there were so few products to choose from). What you buy can have a huge impact on garbage production. Shop for products that will last a long time and that can be repaired if they ever break. Don't buy disposable convenience products. Look for products in recyclable, returnable, or reusable containers. Don't buy products that are overpackaged.

Reuse. Do you have trashy habits? Then think before you dump. Your garbage audit will help you learn what you don't have to toss in the garbage can. All those old things that are cluttering up the garage or basement could be swept off, fixed up a bit, and sold at a garage sale or donated to charitable organizations. Many of these organizations will even come pick them up.

Recycle. Recycling at home and school should be second nature. If your school or neighborhood doesn't have a recycling program, do some research and find out how you can start one. You could even get cash for trash if you pick up aluminum cans and glass bottles that don't find their way into a recycling bin.

Greenpatch Kids

Recycling Researchers

Have you ever wondered how much nonrecyclable and unnecessary garbage is produced by fast-food meals? Erin McClung, Taylor Stokes, and Natalie McCall did. They are ten-year-olds living in Sausalito, California. "We wanted to do this," explains Taylor, "so in a couple of years we're not living in a garbage can." Natalie wanted to do the school-sponsored project so "people will know that they are getting garbage with their fast-food meal." Erin adds, "We can see which fast-food restaurant produces the most garbage so that we don't go there as much."

This intrepid trio ate their way through their project, which they called "Garbage: Inside and Out." Traveling as a team, they had a grown-up drive them to three different fast-food restaurants, where they all purchased a "kid's meal." They ate their meals, saved every scrap of garbage, then returned home. Then they weighed the separate pieces at the local post office and returned to Erin's house to write up the project and analyze the results.

From a total of 36 pieces of garbage—weighing 6.2 ounces—only 3 pieces were made of recycled materials, and 30 pieces could not be recycled! Although there were slight differences in the garbage produced by the three restaurants, they discovered that all three meals produced a lot of nonrecyclable trash.

"All of them had extra packaging for the toys that come with the meals," explained Natalie. "My toy was a straw shaped like a trombone, but at least you could use it again after your meal. The other toys were junk."

"Yeah," says Taylor, "mine was a plastic jumping spider that wouldn't even go an inch high."

Erin's toy was a Sonic Hedgehog. "It was wrapped in plastic, and then, there was another part *inside* that was wrapped in another little plastic bag," says Erin. "They could have just put them together in one bag."

In 1994, Erin, Taylor, and Natalie received a special award for their project from the Marin County Recycling Center. In addition to collecting ribbons, they all received a copy of *50 Simple Things Kids Can Do to Save the Earth*. "I'm glad we did it," says Taylor. "If I have kids when I get older, and I want to know where to eat, I'll probably use this type of information again."

Paper Works

See that old pile of newspapers in the recycle bin? Grab some of it, follow these instructions, and you can make "new" paper from old.

What you need:
piece of wood, ¾ inch square, 3 feet long
handsaw
hammer and nails
measuring tape
window screening, 10 by 8½ inches
blender
water
old paper (computer printout, newspaper, cards)
pan or tub, about 6 inches deep, larger than 10 by 8½ inches
sponge
fibers (vegetable scraps, grass clippings, etc.)
paper towels

1. Saw the wood into two 10-inch pieces and two 7-inch pieces (there will be a little bit of wood left over).
2. Nail the pieces together to make a rectangular frame, approximately 10 by 8½ inches.
3. Nail or staple the window screening to the frame.
4. Fill the blender three-fourths full with water and add scraps of paper. Blend until you create a pulp that is the consistency of a lumpy milkshake. Add about 4 inches of water to your pan. Put two blendersful of this pulp into the pan.
5. To add some texture and color to your paper pulp, you can blend up or chop any of the following fibers and add them to the pan: string, grass clippings, flowers, carrots, beets, or leaves. Be bold and experiment.
6. With one of your hands, mix the pulp and fibers well, then slip the frame into the bottom of the pan, with the flat screen side up. Hold it in place and make sure the pulp is evenly distributed with your other hand. Now, with both hands, slowly lift the screen out of the pan. Keep it level so the pulp is evenly distributed.
7. Drain off excess water and carefully turn the screen over onto some paper towels. Take the sponge and press the back of the screen. Gently lift the screen by one edge and your new sheet of paper will stay on the paper towel. Leave in place until dry.

Resources

Human Anatomy

Your local library or doctor's office will be able to suggest some books if you are interested in how your body works and what it looks like inside. Keep an eye open for the following titles: *The Anatomy Coloring Book* by Wynn Kapit and L. M. Elson, New York: HarperCollins Publishers, 1993; *The Physiology Coloring Book* by Wynn Kapit et al., New York: HarperCollins Publishers, 1987; *The Visual Dictionary of the Human Body*, Eyewitness Visual Dictionaries, London and New York: Dorling Kindersley, 1991. For very detailed information, the following book can probably be found in your library's reference section: *Gray's Anatomy*, Peter L. Williams et al., eds., Edinburgh: Churchill Livingstone, 1989.

Waste Disposal and Recycling

Always begin your information search locally. Call your city or county government and ask if they have an office that coordinates waste disposal or recycling. If they do, call that office and request information. If that doesn't work, write: Solid Waste Assistance Program (SWAP), P.O. Box 7219, Silver Spring, MD 20907. There is also a great video on garbage and recycling called *The Rotten Truth*. It is produced by the Children's Television Workshop. Look for it in your library's video section, your local video store, or write: The Children's Television Workshop, 1 Lincoln Plaza, New York, NY 10023. They also have a toll-free number for ordering: 1-800-321-7511.

If you're interested in starting a school or neighborhood recycling program and obtaining general information about recycling, write: National Recycling Coalition, 1101 30th Street NW #305, Washington, DC 20007.

Storm Drain Pollution and Water Conservation

Contact your city government and local water district to find out if they have educational material regarding storm drain pollution and water conservation. If you can't get anywhere locally, contact The Blue Thumb Club. The Blue Thumb Club has information they can send you on water conservation, protecting water resources, and how to get involved in water issues in your community. Write: American Water Works Association, The Blue Thumb Club, 6666 West Quincy Avenue, Denver, CO 80235.

Plants and Trees

Your library or local botanical garden (many museums and city parks have them) will have loads of information on plants and trees and how to identify them. Look for the following two books: *The Visual Dictionary of Plants*, Eyewitness Visual Dictionaries, New York: Dorling Kindersley, 1992; *Tree*, Eyewitness Books, by David Burnie, New York: Alfred A. Knopf, 1988.

Dermestid Beetles

The Carolina Biological Supply Company sells a "Dermestid Assortment" for $13.95 (item #L885). It includes larvae, pupae, and adult dermestid beetles, and information on how to care for the beetles. Write: Carolina Biological Supply Company, 2700 York Road, Burlington, NC 27215; or call 1-800-334-5551.

Mushrooms

To find out information about mushrooms, the closest mycological society (that's a mushroom club) to you, how you can access mushroom information on your computer, and how to grow mushrooms at home, write: The North American Mycological Association, 3556 Oakwood, Ann Arbor, MI 48104-5213.

To learn about the types of mushrooms that grow around you and how to interpret spore prints, look in your local library for a mushroom guide book. Keep an eye open for: *National Audubon Society Field Guide to North American Mushrooms* by Gary H. Lincoff, New York: Alfred A. Knopf, 1994.

Composting

Start local when it comes to composting and vermi-composting information. Look in gardening magazines, or contact your city or county recycling center and ask for their help. If you can't find any information, look for the following book—it's a fantastic guide to composting, for beginners and advanced composters alike (plus it's funny): *Let It Rot! The home gardener's guide to composting* by Stu Campbell, Pownal, VT: Garden Way Publishing, 1975.

There is also a special publication just for vermi-composting. It contains the latest news on worm composting, book reviews, and a page written just by kids. Write: *Worm Digest*, P.O. Box 544, Eugene, OR 97440.

Parasites

The Center for Disease Control and Prevention (CDC) maintains a Fax Information Service that supplies facsimile documents describing everything from most common parasites to disease risks and outbreaks around the world. All it costs is the price of the telephone call. Call 404-332-4565, and follow the prompts. You need access to a fax machine to use this excellent service. You can also write the CDC and ask them specific questions: CDC, 1600 Clifton Road NE, Atlanta, GA 30333.

Heart Disease

Every state has at least one chapter of the American Heart Association. To find out more information about heart disease and to receive written material, call this telephone number and it will automatically connect you to the chapter closest to you: 1-800-242-8721.

Dying and Death

Your local library will probably have a variety of books discussing dying and death. If you want some serious information, two well-researched books are: *How We Die* by Sherwin B. Nuland, New York: Alfred A. Knopf, 1994, and *Death to Dust* by Kenneth V. Iserson, M.D., Tucson: Galen Press, 1994.

Adopt-a-Species Program

If you live in California or New Mexico, find out about the great "Adopt-a-Species Program" sponsored by the National Audubon Society to help save endangered species and their habitat. You must join this program as a group, and there is an annual prize and award ceremony for the contestants.

California: National Audubon Society; Richardson Bay Audubon Center; 376 Greenwood Beach Rd.; Tiburon, CA 94942; 415-388-2524.

New Mexico: National Audubon Society; Randall Davey Audubon Center; P.O. Box 9314; Santa Fe, NM 87504; 505-983-4609.

Greenpatch Alert:
Endangered and Threatened Species

There are almost 700 animal and plant species listed as threatened or endangered in the U.S. by the federal government (endangered species are worse off than threatened species) and many more worldwide. Endangered or threatened species are "listed" by the federal government only after they are in severe trouble. Scientists must petition the Secretary of the Interior in Washington, D.C., asking that a species be listed. They must provide information on the decline of the species population and the condition of its habitat. If the petition is accepted, then the species becomes a "candidate" for listing as threatened or endangered.

Additionally, state governments have their own rules for listing species. Recovery funds are provided for listed species, and their habitats can be classified as "critical" and more readily preserved. Because of a lack of money and because of political debate, thousands of candidates have yet to be listed.

What You Can Do

If you want to know more about federal endangered species, look for the Greenpatch Alerts in this book, and write the Fish and Wildlife Service at the address below. They can send you a list of all endangered and threatened species, facts about the Endangered Species Act, and information about the recovery programs for listed species.

To find out about endangered species that are only listed by your state, write the Fish and Game Department in your state's capital.

Write to: Division of Endangered Species, U.S. Fish and Wildlife Service, Arlington Square, 4401 N. Fairfax Drive, Arlington, VA 22203. Send a self-addressed, stamped envelope with your letter so it is easier for a representative to write you back.

Glossary

atmosphere the envelope of air surrounding Earth.

autopsy when doctors look inside a corpse to study why a person died. Greek for "seeing with one's own eyes."

autotomy an animal's ability to drop off a body part, for example, lizards' tails. Greek for "self cut."

bolus a small lump of food formed by the mouth before swallowing.

carbon dioxide a gas that humans exhale as a waste product from their lungs after inhaling oxygen. Plants inhale carbon dioxide and exhale oxygen.

carcass the body of a dead animal.

carrion dead, rotting flesh.

castings nutrient-packed worm droppings (feces).

cells the building blocks of life. All living things—people, plants, and animals—are made from cells.

compost the nutrient-rich material that is produced when organic materials are allowed to rot and decompose in place. Compost is an excellent soil additive, and composting is a good way to reduce the amount of garbage going into landfills.

coronary arteries blood vessels in the heart.

corpse a dead body.

cremains human ashes that are placed in a container and either buried, scattered, or put in a columbarium.

cremation a method to dispose of corpses by burning them until nothing but cremains are left. Latin for "to burn."

decomposition the breaking down, or decaying, especially through microbial action.

disease a sickness caused by "germs" (and more formally, "pathogens"), which normally consist of harmful bacteria, viruses, or toxins.

dung animal feces.

ectoparasite a parasite that lives on the skin. *Ecto* is Greek for "outside."

embalming the replacement of a corpse's blood and other fluids with preservative chemicals and disinfectants. It's the most common way to preserve a body for burial in the United States.

endoparasite a parasite that lives in your body. *Endo* is Greek for "within."

epidermis the outermost layer of your skin, which is covered with dead skin cells that are constantly falling off, cell by cell.

feces waste material produced by animals. Packages of waste composed of dead bacteria, dead intestine cells, and tough fibers from meat and plants. The word *feces* typically applies to human waste. *Dung, scat, castings,* or *droppings* are terms used for the feces of other species.

flagella hairlike whips that propel microorganisms, such as bacteria and giardia.

flatus a fancy word for gas ("farts") produced by humans.

follicles the places on your skin where individual hairs grow.

fungus important decomposers and digesters of the forest floor. Mushrooms are the best-known type of fungus. Fungi survive by being parasitic, saprophytic, or by forming symbiotic relationships with plants.

heart disease a disease or abnormal condition of the heart.

hypertrophy the ability for human organs to enlarge in size without additional cell production.

landfills what today's garbage dumps are called. Landfills are engineered to minimize pollution and to be covered with dirt when full.

leaf litter a mix of decomposing leaves, twigs, and animal droppings on top of the soil.

mitosis the process by which cells divide into exact copies of themselves.

morticians the professionals who prepare corpses for burial or cremation, also known as undertakers or funeral directors.

mycophagist someone who eats wild mushrooms.

nits the eggs of female lice. They are laid at the base of hair follicles.

ovum a single-celled egg produced by female animals that when fertilized by male sperm, develop into embryos and eventually babies.

parasite a plant or animal species that lives on or in other living species.

photosynthesis the process by which plants store solar energy with the help of a chemical called chlorophyll. This stored energy makes carbohydrates from carbon dioxide and water. Carbohydrates are important sources of nourishment for all living things. Greek for "light" and "to put together."

pus a mixture of dead tissue, bacterial cells, and living and dead WBCs that form a gooey liquid around cuts.

red blood cells (RBCs) the cells that carry oxygen from your lungs to your body's tissues and exchange it for carbon dioxide.

rigor mortis the stiffening of a corpse several hours after death.

roadkill dead animals found on roads, usually killed by traffic.

saprophytic when a species lives on or in another species without killing it.

scabs blood cells that dry and die over wounds until they heal.

scavenger species that eat carrion; for example, turkey vultures, which eat roadkills.

sperm a single cell produced by male animals that can fertilize an ovum.

storm drain pollution when pollutants are dumped in the gutter, or down a storm drain, or rain picks up oil and pollution from the street, and the runoff pours into the local waterway without being cleaned.

symbiosis when a species lives on or in another species while helping that species to survive. A mutually beneficial relationship.

totipotent the ability of plants to grow roots from the open end of a cutting.

urine waste material produced by animals. Urine in humans is mostly extra water, urea (a compound formed by the decomposition of protein), and salt.

vermi-compost composting with worms. *Vermi* is Latin for "worm."

white blood cells (WBCs) cells that are like internal scavengers you carry around with you at all times. WBCs move throughout your body searching out bacteria.

zygote an ovum that was fertilized by a sperm. Zygotes divide into 2 cells one day after fertilization is completed, then 8 cells after three days, then 64 cells after four days.

Index

Acknowledgments

The author received help from many people: Peter Gebbie, Dr. Richard Leahy, and Dr. Isaac Silberman (biology, medicine, dying, and death); Cortney Cassidy, Ruth Gravanis, Mike Herz, Tom Mumley, and Joan Patton (storm drain pollution and water issues); Allen Hersch (toxic waste); Dr. Harry Greene (animals); Mark Bowers and Nadine Hardin (garbage and recycling); Dr. Kenneth Cochran (mushrooms); Jan Knight (botany); Carl Grimm and Steve Sherman (composting); and Jeanne Tinsman (condors). And, as usual, the staff members of my hometown library in Mill Valley, California, were informative and encouraging throughout. Thank you one and all.

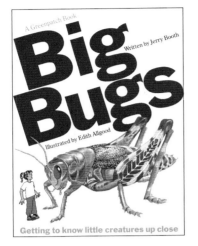

The Greenpatch Kids Want You!

All over the world, this very minute, kids just like you are working to make the earth a safe place for all living things. There is a lot to do. You and your friends can help. If you do, you will be joining hundreds and thousands of kids everywhere. Here are some ways you can get started:

1. Join the Greenpatch Kids.

The Greenpatch Kids is an alliance of young people who want to learn about the environment and how to protect it. Anyone can join. If your copy of this book includes a mail-back card, complete the form with your name and address, and send it in. (Don't forget a stamp.) If there isn't a card in your book, write your name, address, age, and school on a piece of paper, put it in an envelope, and send it to the address below. You will receive a Greenpatch membership card and a free copy of the *Greenpatch News*, which is full of ideas for projects and will tell you what other kids are doing. Write to:

**Greenpatch Kids
Harcourt Brace Children's Books
525 B Street, Suite 1900
San Diego, CA 92101**

2. Start a Greenpatch Kids group.

Governments and big environmental groups can't always work in your neighborhood, but you and your friends sure can! All you need is an adult sponsor, some friends, and a plan.

Do a neighborhood bio-survey. What animals and plants live there? Are any of them endangered? What can you do to protect them? Start a pollution watch. The health of our earth *starts in your neighborhood.*

3. Tell us about your project.

The people who made this book and Greenpatch Kids everywhere want to know what you are doing. Your idea might be just what someone else needs. If you have a project that works, send us a description. Be sure to include your name, address, age, and telephone number, in case we need to contact you for more information.

4. Contact and work with other groups.

To get help for your project, or to find out what to do in your neighborhood, contact other groups. The largest environmental group for young people is *Kids for Saving Earth*. It costs $7 to join (or $15 for your group), but they will send you a free information pack if you write or call them. Ask them if there is already a KSE group in your town. Write *Kids for Saving Earth*, P.O. Box 47247, Plymouth, MN 55447, or phone 612-525-0002.